T0316779

Jacint Verdaguer
Mount Canigó

Jacint Verdaguer
Mount Canigó

A tale of Catalonia

Introduction and translation by
Ronald Puppo

BARCINO·TAMESIS
BARCELONA/WOODBRIDGE 2015

© Introduction and translation, Ronald Puppo, 2015

All Rights Reserved. Except as permitted under current legislation no part of this work may be photocopied, stored in a retrieval system, published, performed in public, adapted, broadcast, transmitted, recorded or reproduced in any form or by any means, without the prior permission of the copyright owner.

First published 2015
by Tamesis (Serie B: TEXTOS, 59)
in association with Editorial Barcino

LLLL institut
ramon llull
Catalan Language and Culture

The translation of this work has been supported by a grant from the Institut Ramon Llull

ISBN 978 1 85566 298 8
COPYRIGHT DEPOSIT: B. 21336-2015

Tamesis is an imprint of Boydell & Brewer Ltd
PO Box 9, Woodbridge, Suffolk IP12 3DF, UK
and of Boydell & Brewer Inc.
668 Mt Hope Avenue, Rochester, NY 14620, USA
www.boydellandbrewer.com

Editorial Barcino, S. A.
Acàcies 15. 08027 Barcelona, Spain
www.editorialbarcino.cat

The English translations of "La Maladeta," "Guisla" and "The Two Bell Towers" were first published in *Selected Poems of Jacint Verdaguer: A Bilingual Edition*, copyright © 2007 by The University of Chicago, with whose kind permission they are reproduced here.

Designed and typeset by Jordi Casas

Printed in Spain by Gràfiko

Cover illustration:
Adrià Gual, *The Dew*
Detail, Oil on canvas, 1897
© MNAC - Museu Nacional d'Art de Catalunya
Barcelona, 2015
Foto: Calveras/Mérida/Sagristà

Contents

Introduction, 7
References, 23

Mount Canigó

Canto I. The Gathering, 27
Canto II. Flordeneu, 39
Canto III. Enchantment, 49
Canto IV. The Pyrenees, 61
Canto V. Tallaferro, 79
Canto VI. Nuptials, 87
Canto VII. Disenchantment, 107
Canto VIII. The Giant's Pit, 129
Canto IX. The Burial, 135
Canto X. Guisla, 155
Canto XI. Oliba, 163
Canto XII. The Cross of Canigó, 177
Epilogue. The Two Bell Towers, 197

Annotated index, 203

Introduction

To LOOK OUT at the easternmost Pyrenees from the plains below and to see, in the early spring or late autumn, the Canigó massif with its tapering snow-topped summits silhouetted by a blue sky, is to invite the imagination to match all their wonder and majesty with a tale whose scope and depth will be equal to the epic magnitude of the mountains themselves. It must be a tale of love, of loyalty, of faith, of change and yet permanence, of sacred bonds broken and renewed, of transgression and reconciliation, of tragedy and yet of hope; and it must transcend the bounds of the individual actors whose stories are played out, weaving the history and geography of people and of peoples into the fabric of the narrative tapestry, entifying the events of a particular time and place while at the same time airlifting them, through the discursive magic of storytelling, across the barriers of time and space and into the hearts of everyone, everywhere.

Jacint Verdaguer's *Mount Canigó: A Tale of Catalonia* is, and does, just that. Extracting and shaping the raw material for the telling — drawn both from the land itself and from the people it sustains — the poet blends life and legend into an epic foundational mix, enlarging the events and the pathos trailing in their wake, and peopling the land with the men and women who have through generations inscribed the mountainscapes not only with the divine presence of their faith — "Clad in rags (guise He takes to walk the world), / He called one evening at some shepherds' hut" (canto 4) — but also with the magical beings of their ancient lore: Pyrenean faeries, whose magnificent mountain halls the poet opens for all to see — "Inside, a hundred corridors / branch out like city avenues, / each strewn with lights in shimmering colors / that glaze the clay like pearls of dew" (canto 6).

Acclaimed throughout Europe soon after its publication in 1886, the 4378-line poetic narrative is set in eleventh-century Catalonia, mostly on the French side in what is today the region of Rosselló (Fr. Roussillon) during the Christian reconquest of the Spanish March, today Catalonia. The waging of war between Christians and Saracens — recalling the heroic Roland (whose memory is evoked no less than five times in the narrative) — is interlaced with an intracultural clash between a folk mythology rooted in the natural geography, where the Pyrenean faeries reign supreme, and the broadly institutionalized hegemony of early medieval Christendom. Three of the protagonists central to the unfolding of both these conflicts are actual historical figures: Count Bernat of Besalú (aka Tallaferro) and his two brothers, Count Guifre of Cerdanya, and Bishop-Abbot Oliba of Vic and Santa Maria de Ripoll. The outstanding and tragic figure of the story, however, is the fictional character of the young Gentil, newly knighted, who falls in love with Griselda, a shepherdess, thereby transgressing the mores of his station and rousing the anger of his father, Count Tallaferro. Commanding a militia against the Saracen advance, Gentil is soon drawn from his post by the promise of fulfillment with the help of the mountain's magic; reaching the summits, he encounters Flordeneu, queen of the Pyrenean faeries, who deceives him by taking on the appearance of Griselda, and would carry him off for herself. Gentil, high on the mountain, is torn between heart and honor, but already it is too late: "Alas! inside Gentil's unseasoned heart / Now clash in ruthless combat love and land: / And when stern love assaults a tender heart, / Not always is it duty that endures" (canto 2).

MANY TALES

Many are the tales within the tale. Counterpointing throughout the fourfold dramatic arc Gentil-Tallaferro-Guifre-Oliba is a storyteller's treasure-trove of narrative polyphony. Perhaps the most striking of these tangential stories are the three recounted by the faeries themselves to delight Gentil while their queen readies herself for the wedding (canto 7). In the first of these three stories, more than one hundred lines are given voice by the Faerie of Mirmanda, who relates Hannibal's thundering passage across the Pyrenees on his way to Cannae: "One hundred elephants follow — like marching / peaks, great silhouettes on the Pyrenees' back: / three-hundred-year oaks bow to let them pass, / while chestnuts crack beneath their mammoth feet. / And on the highest, inside a sculpted tower, / sits Hannibal — riding the sprawling peaks. / Seeing him out of the clouds, were I not faerie, / I'd have bent my knee as before a god." The second is a playful tale of two rivers, told by the Faerie of Fontargent, about how the Noguera and the Garona spring from the same valley, but one flows southward and one northward: "A Spaniard frenchified, / Garona, paltry patriot, / carries off to France / his wealth acquired in Spain; / and seeing us poor in springs, / spills wide into the Atlantic, / while the other, scant and salty, / trickles into the Mediterranean." Finally, the Faerie of Lanós tells the tragic tale of Lampegia, daughter of Duke Eudes I (aka Odo the Great) of Aquitaine (died c. 735), and how Lampegia's wedlock with the rebel governor of Cerdanya, Abu-Nezah (or Munuza), sealed a peace between Islam and Christendom — only to be broken by Abd ar-Rahman's invading army, who now put Abu-Nezah to death and abduct Lampegia; this same army will be subsequently defeated by Charles Martel at the Battle of Tours in 732. (Verdaguer draws here from the nineteenth-century Catalan poet, chronicler and statesman Víctor Balaguer [1860: 171-172]; the events are also chronicled by Enlightenment historian Edward Gibbon [1825: 467-480].)

Another tale of special importance is "Eixalada," told by Oliba (canto 9), and within which is embedded the account of the destruction by flooding of the monastery at Eixalada, as told by the few monks who survived the disaster at the court of Charlemagne in Aquae Grani. The significance of the tale is twofold. First, it will be these same surviving monks who go on to establish a new Benedictine abbey at Sant Miquel de Cuixà under the auspices of Charlemagne, which will in turn serve as seedbed for the new abbey, Sant Martí del Canigó, to be erected further up the mountain by Oliba at the request of Guifre, who vows to live out his days there in penitence for his crime; Guifre will bid farewell to his wife with these words: "And I will always love you, just as ever, / But it must be, alas! from a monk's cell / Inside a cloister to be raised above / The shrine of Sant Martí del Canigó. / There I should have left this life, on the gallows, / Between the earth and sky, devoured by crows; / Through God's compassion I am granted life: / To Him I mean to render its remainder!" (canto 10). Second, the legendary knight Enveig, responsible for the destruction of the abbey at Eixalada (though it was the vengeful Faerie of Lanós who set the scheme into motion), will, as Ricard Torrents has noted (1995, 226-227), serve Verdaguer as a crude template for his fictional character of Gentil.

In another tale within the tale, Flordeneu gives voice to seventy-five of one hundred twenty lines under the title "Rosselló" (canto

6), evoking the region's natural, legendary and human geographies throughout the ages: "'Long this vale lay hid from view,' says the Faerie, / 'What's grass was water: all that's green was blue; / Whales once sang where the town of Prada stands, / And Elna's cloisters cap the coral-pink / Ivory palace of Tethys.'" Recalled also is the ebb and flow of civilizations that visit and settle Rosselló's shores; among these: "Phoenicians founded cities on her shores, / Yet, wandering spouse in search of other bed, / Kissed her walls one thousand years — then left; / Their gaze and tunics blue all gone from sight, / The walls gave way to heartbreak."

Surely the most curious of all inlaid tales is "A Saint John's Bouquet" (canto 1), recounted by a jongleur bent on stirring up trouble between the lads of the plains and the mountains, and whose song — tracing the origins of the custom of putting a bouquet of wildflowers on one's door on Midsummer's Day (the Feast of Saint John) — identifies the mountain lads, renowned as firespinners (adept at dancing with firebrands), with the Devil, who in the song takes the form of a firespinner appearing to a Pyrenean maid, whose only protection is the bouquet she has hung on her door; foiled, her diabolical suitor reveals himself. (See the final section of this introduction: "The translation.")

A number of other inset stories, shorter, punctuate the narrative throughout. At times it is a character who gives them voice, as when Flordeneu tells of the popular origin of the city of Perpinyà (Fr. Perpignan), founded by a mountain-dwelling plowman, Pere Pinya, who asks the River Tet to lead him down to the warm and fertile plain near the sea: "When at last they reached a spot near the sea, / The river said, 'Settle here, plow and plant — / I shall water your fields.' // "Like Romulus one day along the Tiber, / He staked a plot out with his ash wood cart; / There he set a house, field, and olive tree; / And now the house is town, broad walls the cart-tracks — / Broad walls of Perpinyà" (canto 6); or as when a messenger arrives with the news of Tallaferro's death in the swelling waters of the Rhone: "Searching and reaching for his struggling steed, / The weight of his armor pulling him under, / He floundered and gasped, and grappled with death. / An hour went by, and on that fatal bank, / In the shade of a willow's greeny tresses, / My deceased seigneur slept his final sleep" (canto 11). At other times, the narrator directly inlays a brief tale, telling, for instance, how Saint William of Combret, mocked by the uncooperative bellsmiths of Montferrer, molded the iron bell for his chapel with his bare hands; "'It boils in the forge!' they mock. 'Take it! It's yours!' / So the good saint plunges his hands in the melt, / molding the mix like a potter his clay, / and curving the flare in the form of a miter. / He honors today that promise he made, / tolling the tempest, and foes that press near" (canto 5); or how the ungenerous shepherds and their flocks were turned into features of the landscape as a reminder to others: "Behind, he saw the mountain pastures empty: / The cliffs above stood out as sheep and lambs, / Rocks now formed by kids, goats, and shepherd dogs; / And their shepherds, remaining to this day, / All turned, they too, to rock" (canto 4).

Such is the scope and depth of the epic narrative — enriched by the abundance of history and legend and lore that springs from the Pyrenees and its environs. Verdaguer himself gleaned this striking wealth of natural and human geography from the landscape and its people during his extensive summer travels on foot throughout the Catalan Pyrenees between 1879 and 1883, including several ascents to the summit of Canigó (9,137 ft) and various other ascents to the highest peaks in the eastern Pyrenees: Puigmal (9,547 ft), Carlit (9,583 ft), La Pica d'Estats (10,311 ft), La Maladeta (10,853 ft), and Aneto (11,168 ft); many of these vigorous travels are recorded by Verdaguer in his *Excursions i viatges* (Excursions and Travels, 1887).

THE TWO BELL TOWERS

The telescoped time of the narrative retracts swiftly into Verdaguer's own day in the poem's crowning epilogue, "The Two Bell Towers," in which the poet gives voice to the bell towers of the two abandoned abbeys now fallen into ruin, Sant Miquel de Cuixà and Sant Martí del Canigó. Surveying the crumbling remains on the desolate landscape, the towers strike up a conversation but see little hope of reversing their decline. The final lines of their exchange are spoken by the tower of Cuixà: "And soon my skeleton, deformed and wrecked, / Will lie undone and bleached in Codalet; / My head weighs heavy, and with night advancing, / When rising up to make her vesper visit, / The moon marvels to find me here still standing. // I too will go and rest, and from your hilltop / You too one day will join me on this spot, / And those whose plows above our graves make good / Will never say, nor guess, what was our lot, / Where Sant Miquel and Sant Martí once stood." Nevertheless, as pointed out elsewhere (Puppo 2012: 118), the decline and impending rift between past and future in an uncertain present are transcended in the poem's final lines by what Ricard Torrents, and separately, Arthur Terry, have suggested is a "telluric" or geographic identity (Torrents 2004: 132; Terry 2003: 65), signaling the role — both vital and symbolic — of the landscape interacting with the human geography. The poem's concluding stanzas read: "So spoke the pair of belfries there that night; / But next day, at dawn, in the morning sunlight. / Taking up the strains left off in the vale, / The ringdove stopped to converse with the ivy, / The daystar to chat with the nightingale. // Heartened, the mountain smiled down on the scene, / And boasting a burgeoning cloak of green, / Shone like a bride all decked with jewels and gems, / Then doffed a thousand snowdrifts from its mien / Just like an orange sapling snowy blossoms. // What one century builds up, the next brings low, / But God's enduring monument stands long: / Nor raging winds, nor war, nor wrath of men / Will overturn the peaks of Canigó: / The soaring Pyrenees will not be bent." The symbolic force conferred here on the landscape, and infused also into the spirit of the people who inhabit it through a collective memory of events played out on a shared natural and human geography — events reenacted and celebrated through the medium of the poem itself — is, as Torrents has noted, what makes *Mount Canigó* the foundational poem of the Catalan people (2004: 133); and although Verdaguer, writing in the nineteenth century, posited a people cemented together by the principles of Christian faith (Verdaguer was, after all, a Catholic priest), the poem's symbolic potential points to the realization that the ingredients of nation-building may change with the centuries. Significantly, the statement attributed to Bishop Josep Torras i Bages (1846-1916), that "Catalonia will be Christian or not at all," may be reformulated, Torrents suggests, as "Catalonia will be — even if not Christian" (132). What might be today the determining factors of national identity? Torrents reflects on this:

> The debate over Catalan identity is none other than a particular instance of the general debate over the identities of Europe [...] In fact, Europe is a sum of identities where each country participates in the particular and the general debate on two fronts: the

historical, weighing in the avatars of identities throughout the existence of the entity Europe; and the up-to-date, putting shifting contemporary identities on the table, antagonistic and assimilative alike, resulting from extra-European immigration, political alliances, cultural interchange and globalizing policies. (120)

The strength of *Mount Canigó* as the enduring nineteenth-century foundational poem of the Catalan people stands largely on this epilogue, "The Two Bell Towers," added to the second edition (1901), but missing from the first edition (1886), which closes with the triumphant planting of the cross on the summit and the driving away of the faeries (canto 12). The inclusion of the epilogue, Torrents argues, recasts the ending of *Mount Canigó*, changing it from *hymnal* to *elegiac*; the story is now open-ended, and how the story of the people symbolically embodied in Verdaguer's foundational epic will turn out, only the future can say: "As long as Mt. Canigó continues to stand, so too will stand *Mount Canigó*, the poem, and the land to which it continually gives rise. It is works of literature that are the homeland of peoples with no sovereign state" (2003: 245).

First published as a separate poem in 1887 (subsequent to the appearance of *Canigó*), Verdaguer would later reveal how the stanzas of "The Two Bell Towers" were the first of the legendary epic to be written, and as "the [*Canigó*] project grew bigger, they were left outside the edifice, piled aside like leftover stones" (quoted in Pinyol 2002: 173); the restoration of the monastery at Santa Maria de Ripoll just undertaken by Bishop Josep Morgades (1826-1901) had all but eclipsed the role of the abandoned abbeys of Cuixà and Canigó in the longer poem, whose canto eleven, "Oliba," Verdaguer dedicated to Morgades — the restoration itself an echo of the triumphant reconstruction of the Ripoll abbey impelled by Morgades's medieval forerunner, Oliba. Still, it should be noted that for the French translation of *Canigó* published in 1889, translator Josep Tolrà de Bordas obtained Verdaguer's permission to include "The Two Bell Towers" as the epilogue, prefiguring in the French version Verdaguer's inclusion of it in the second and definitive 1901 Catalan edition (see Pinyol 2002: 176-177; see Vilardell Domènech 2013 on the numerous translations of *Canigó* into Spanish). Meanwhile, the curious chain of events leading to Verdaguer's estrangement from the bishop (who would suspend Verdaguer's duties and functions as a priest in 1895,

prompting a counterattack by Verdaguer in a series of articles published in Barcelona's left-leaning press — sparking the highly publi-
cized Verdaguer-Morgades clash that sent repercussions rippling
throughout Spain and abroad, and polarizing Catalan society so sharply that the scars of the trauma remain to this day [see Torrents 2003:
243-244]) and, conversely, the steps taken by Bishop Juli Carsalade du
Pont (1847-1932), bishop of Perpignan, to initiate the reconstruction
of the Canigó and Cuixà abbeys, would cause Verdaguer to retract the
dedication to Morgades and dedicate the second edition of *Canigó*
to Carsalade and the "Catalans of France" (see Torrents 2003: 244;
Pinyol 2002: 178). (Verdaguer's priestly duties would be reinstated
by 1898, thanks largely to the conciliating efforts of the Augustinian
friars at El Escorial, Madrid; for a thoroughgoing English-language
biographical sketch of Verdaguer, see Pinyol 2007: 2-17.)

A POET-PRIEST'S LEGACY

Renowned chiefly for his foundational poetic narratives of Spain and
Catalonia — *L'Atlàntida* (1877) and *Canigó* (1886) — Verdaguer, with
his vast production of lyric and epic poetry, his immensely popular
appeal at home, and his swift ascent to recognition throughout Spain
and abroad would come to trigger an exponential impact on the state
of Catalan letters, given the circumstance that Verdaguer stepped
onto the scene at just the critical moment — a decisive crossroads in
the life of the Catalan language and the fulfillment of its potential as
an effective vehicle for written culture — ushering in literary Catalan's
road to recovery in the second half of the nineteenth century.

The spark set off in Verdaguer's imagination by the ancient tale
of the destruction of Atlantis, and concomitantly, Columbus's first
voyage and the emergence of an uncharted world to the west began
to take poetic form in his days as a seminarian in Vic. *L'Atlàntida*
would appear nine years later, after long and substantial revision and,
seasonably, the two years spent by Verdaguer making nine round-trip
crossings of the Atlantic as chaplain on the transatlantic ships of his
patron, the self-made shipping mogul and financier Antonio López,
possessor in his day of the largest personal fortune in Spain (see
Pinyol 2007: 4). Hailed as the epic that would restore Catalan literature's rank among the literatures of Europe after a hiatus of some

three centuries (Frederic Mistral compared it to John Milton's *Paradise Lost* and Alphonse de Lamartine's *La chute d'un ange*), *L'Atlàntida* fuses the heroism of Hercules with Judeo-Christian providentialism. On the one hand, the poem recasts Hercules's labors linked to the Iberian Peninsula — the encounter with Geryon, Hesperides and the golden apples (in Verdaguer's account an orange tree), the opening of the Strait of Gibraltar, the founding of Barcelona — and to top it off, Hercules, by wedlock with Hesperis (the widowed queen of Atlantis), appears as the progenitor of a new Iberian people. On the other hand, Columbus's bridging of the Atlantic opens the way for the spread of Catholicism, which, Torrents observes, is "the first ideology of globalization" (2004: 105). With the continents again united by Columbus, the "pattern of cosmic retribution and renewal" is, following Terry (2003: 63), now complete, and Spain, as noted by Pere Farrés, has fulfilled "[its] destiny in the transmittance of Christianity" (2003: 70). Numerous translations of *L'Atlàntida* soon appeared in several European languages: Spanish, French (see Camps Casals 2013), Italian, German, Czech, and Portuguese; of the English translation undertaken by Verdaguer's Irish contemporary William Bonaparte-Wyse (1826-1892), only two fragments were completed prior to the translator's death: "Introduction" and "Isabella's Dream" (both included in Puppo 2007: 36-51).

As pointed out elsewhere (Puppo 2010: 264-271), Verdaguer's remarkable poetic achievement spans a wide range of prominent themes of enduring symbolic significance which, rooted in the particulars of his time and place, are raised lyrically and epically to universal stature and appeal. Verdaguer's poetic accounts of Christian martyrdom, drawn from historical and legendary sources, may take on the epic tone of his *Dos màrtirs de ma pàtria* (Two Christian Martyrs of Ausona, 1865), or, alternatively, the more intimist rendering of the Saint Eulària tradition in *Martiri* (Martyrdom, 1899). Again fusing faith and tradition, it was Verdaguer who poeticized the history and spirituality of Montserrat Abbey, from its legendary origins and St. Ignatius of Loyola's famed visit to the abbey on 25 March 1522 to its destruction by Napoleon's troops in 1811-12 and the triumphal return of the Benedictines to Montserrat in 1844; his long poem *Llegenda de Montserrat* (Legend of Montserrat, 1880) and *Cançons de Montserrat* (Songs of Montserrat, 1880) shone as the literary keystone of the monastery's 1880 millennial celebrations that ran for two years, during which the Black Madonna of Montserrat (La Moreneta) was solemnly proclaimed Patroness of Catalonia by the Vatican in 1881. Saint Francis of Assisi holds also a prominent place in Verdaguer: written over a span of twenty-six years, the Saint Francis poems in *Sant Francesc* (1895) reveal a development in Verdaguer's relationship with the Franciscan tradition marked by what Isidor Cònsul (2001: 17-65) has identified as three salient moments in the poet's life, culminating in the mounting conflict with Bishop Morgades and Verdaguer's feeling that, as the poet notes in his prologue to the volume, his own tribulations parallel in some ways those of the early-thirteenth-century ascetic whom he so admired. As for Verdaguer's most outstanding among many poetic invocations of Barcelona, *A Barcelona* (To Barcelona, 1883), it would set into motion "a strange and highly productive series of visions of [Barcelona's] greatness" that came to enlist over the following century responses from the pens of no less than fifteen major Catalan poets (Bou 1991: 16-17).

To capture the complete picture of Verdaguer's accomplishment is, writes Lluís Solà, notoriously difficult: "All too quickly did [Verdaguer's] work appear where no one expected it, and all too vertically did it rise from that which, with its appearance, was now indisputable: a renaissance" (2013: 15). Verdaguer's was "the task of celebrating the ceremony of origins, the foundation and the founding of these origins, the carrying out of the renaissance, the rebirth." Solà goes on to underscore the danger of unremembrance: "At each historical moment, at each now and each place, there must begin inexorably the ceremony of renewal and rebirth, and it is poetry that is [its] substance." Verdaguer's was, moreover, "a twofold renaissance [since it] was not possible to renew the land without renewing the language, nor was it possible to renew the language without renewing the land" (18). The poet's ability to renew the language and the land is, we may recall, powerfully encapsulated in "The Two Bell Towers," prelude to the renewal and reconstruction of the Canigó and Cuixà abbeys at the very moment their decline and disappearance seemed all but inevitable.

Perhaps the magnitude of Verdaguer's literary accomplishment, and the social, and ultimately political, repercussions of cultural and national renewal that would touch the hearts and imaginations of a people whose peripheral collective body was in decline, and all but invisible amid the pandemic cultural daltonism that screens so many peoples from global view, perhaps all this may strike us as incongruous with Verdaguer's ecclesiastical station in life. What, we might ask, is he doing so far beyond the conventional confines that define the obligations and suitable activities of a priest? We might ask the same question of any number of persons who have committed themselves to their religious calling, and yet whose abilities and aspirations have drawn them beyond the narrow confines of their conventional role and set them squarely in the face of the headwinds of their peoples' histories.

THE TRANSLATION

Perhaps the most striking feature of *Canigó*'s original Catalan verse is its metrically variegated form, the versification in each of the twelve cantos and epilogue varying with the poetic narrative's shifting themes and tone. For instance, cantos five and eight, fraught with battle, resemble the *laisses* of the Old French chanson de geste, roughly comparable to the alliterative verse of the Anglo-Saxon epic, while the melodic vignettes depicting Flordeneu's palace in cantos three and six deploy rhyming quatrains that evoke the English Romantics; at other times, as in the dramatically-paced flow of cantos two and ten, Verdaguer's non-stanzaic decasyllables recall the lyrical virtuosity of Tennyson, while his masterful Catalan alexandrines (dodecasyllables feminine at the caesura) mirror the mountains' majesty in "La Maladeta" and "Rosselló" (cantos four and six) with their potently packed imagery unfolding into sestets and cinquains, respectively, with each stanza thrown into rhythmic relief by its final half-line coda.

Our aim, as in the *Selected Poems* (see Puppo, 2007, 21-23), has been to render Verdaguer into rhythmic, readable, modern English verse; as discussed elsewhere, this involves re-creating an English-language form-content synthesis that seeks to approximate the rhythm and tone of the original Catalan (though departing from it, too, at times) in such a way that might "evoke familiar and parallel resonance in Verdaguer's translator-mediated readership" (Puppo 2012: 109). For example, Verdaguer's rhyming alexandrines (dodecasyllables) and half-line codas in "La Maladeta" are rendered in non-rhyming iambic pentameter (with some variation) and a final trimeter: "Years passed, centuries piled on centuries / Before this bone-frame of primeval giants / Dressed itself in topsoil and timberland, / Before

the crags grew moss, the meadows flowers, / Before the forests filled
with thronging birds, / The thronging birds with song" (canto 4).
Here, and throughout the poem, slant rhyme, internal rhyme, weak
rhyme, assonance, alliteration, and other rhythmic elements combine
to balance and compensate where it has not always been possible to
reproduce the Catalan end rhyme.

In addition to repackaging Verdaguer's poetics with a view to
resolving lyrical and metrical issues, lexical problems, too, arise.
Again, as pointed out elsewhere, I discovered a good number of intertextual correspondences with works of poetic narrative in English,
or in English translation, that proved decisive in dealing with many
lexical challenges. Particularly invaluable were intertextual correspondences found in Spenser's *Faerie Queene*, Ariosto's *Orlando Furioso*
(in Guido Waldman's translation), Milton's *Paradise Lost*, Tennyson's
Idylls of the King, and Longfellow's *Evangeline* and *The Song of Hiawatha*
(2012: 108-118). To cite just one example here: Longfellow provided
me with a solution to the problem of translating the Catalan word *jai*
("old man" or "grandfather") as a personification of the Pyrenean
peak known as Alp in canto four. Not very satisfied with the diction-
ary equivalents found for *jai*, I later recalled a poem that Longfellow
wrote about his grandchildren, "The Children's Hour," in which the
children descend on the poet from upstairs, devouring him with hugs
and kisses. Longfellow uses the figure of synecdoche, taking his own
mustache as the identifying element: "Do you think, O blue-eyed
banditti, / because you have scaled the wall, / such an old mustache
as I am / is not a match for you all!" (Longfellow, 1988, 371); so by
rendering *jai* using the suitable identifying element here — "an old
bald head" — Verdaguer's lines find a lyrical expression in English
that rings true in its emotive tone: "Then Alp, an old bald head
assailed by children, / stoops, gigantic, beneath their golden coach: /
a ring of timbering pines all round his peak, / just like the tonsured
top upon a monk" (canto 4).

Other types of intertextual correspondences have also arisen in
the course of giving voice to Verdaguer in English. Longfellow's
book-length poem *The Song of Hiawatha* served as a metrical template for translating the 136-line stretch of verse titled "Lampegia"
(canto 7): recast in the same meter (trochaic tetrameter) that
takes Longfellow's readers back to the legendary past of Hiawatha's
exploits, Lampegia's story, retold and revoiced in English, resonates

with this newfound intertextual correspondence, exemplifying what I have called *translative intertextuality*, that is, an instance of new correspondence to intertextual others in the translating, or receptor, literary system (2012: 108-118); Longfellow's Hiawathan meter was itself adapted from the Finnish epic *The Kalevala* (see Aaron 1992: xi-xii), adding a further layer, here, of cross-cultural intertextual correspondence.

The greatest departure in my rendering of Verdaguer's *Canigó* occurs in "A Saint John's Bouquet" (canto 1), where I admittedly test the bounds of what have been called "writerly" decisions taken by translators (see Bush 2006) which give rise to meanings not expressed — at least not explicitly — in the original work, but without which the translation may fall short of its potential as a text which, in addition to being a representation of the original work, is also, arguably, a text in itself (see Koster 2002). In my expanded textual characterization I make it clear that the Devil is a slick charmer, whose glib discourse will delight the modern reader: "Yes, turtledove, some might say I was — well, / high placed, / but then (though I hadn't quite thought you could tell), / things didn't work out as I'd planned, and I fell — / from grace. / So now I'm in charge of alternative lifestyles / instead. / Were it not for this posy, you'd be my new wife: / with an excellent view of the brimstony miles — / round my bed." My contention here is that an unexpanded rendering of the Devil would strip him of his intellectual and rhetorical powers; by writing the Devil's character I am simply connecting the dots — to do otherwise would be a disservice to the poetic narrative and, ultimately, Verdaguer. Separately, and importantly, this conspicuous depiction of the Devil as a slick customer connects firmly with Verdaguer's "strange" period when from 1891 to 1893 he participated in the performing of exorcisms, in which the alleged speech of demons through allegedly possessed persons was recorded by Verdaguer in several notebooks (see Junyent 1994, Soberanas 2002 and Casasses 2014); to give one example: "in the Church all are sleeping, even His Holiness is asleep;" thus, the ecclesiastic hierarchy and the authenticity of its commitment are candidly mocked by an astute Devil, and since the Church has fallen under his spell, it is to the customs and remedies of everyday life that the common people must turn: the Pyrenean maid keeps the Devil effectively at bay with a simple bouquet of wildflowers.

George Steiner has remarked that "translation is the donation of being across space and time" (1996, 202). This culturally specific, lowercased being becomes, in the textual and contextual transformation that is translation, a catalyst for encounter beyond the cultural self — leaping across linguistic and cultural boundaries, we come to realize that the only truly insurmountable limits when it comes to literary translation, that is, in giving new voice to otherly voices and carrying them across (*trans* + *latus*) time and space, would be the fading away of the voices themselves (see Puppo 2012: 120-121).

I am deeply indebted to a number of Verdaguerian scholars who have helped me in countless ways during my encounter with Catalonia's poet of poets over the past two decades, particularly Ricard Torrents, Ramon Pinyol, Francesc Codina, Lluís Solà, M. Àngels Verdaguer, M. Carme Bernal, Llorenç Soldevila, and Carme Torrents (director of the Casa Museu Verdaguer / Fundació Jacint Verdaguer, Folgueroles). I am especially indebted to the late Arthur Terry of the University of Essex (who in my early attempts at translating Verdaguer succeeded in weaning me away from hopelessly archaic renderings) and to the late Segimon Serrallonga of the Universitat de Vic, both of whose wisdom and generous guidance have made this translation possible at all, and to whose memory it is dedicated. I am also indebted to the highly accomplished literary translator Peter Bush, whose careful and critical reading of my translation helped smooth over some rough edges; any remaining flaws are the result of my own shortcomings in judgment. My heartfelt thanks also to Carles Duarte and Joan Santanach of Editorial Barcino.

Special mention must be made here of James Wm. Millard, MCIL, whose long labor of love produced the first nearly complete English translation of Verdaguer's *Canigó* under the title *Canigó, A Legend of the Pyrenees* (Cleveleys: Ibertext, 2000); though not for sale to the public, the edition was made available free of charge to school libraries in the U.K.

My annotated translations of "La Maladeta," "Guisla" and "The Two Bell Towers" were first published in *Selected Poems of Jacint Verdaguer. A Bilingual Edition*, copyright © 2007 by The University of Chicago, with whose kind permission they are reproduced here. Separately, "A Saint John's Bouquet" was published as "Midsummer

Bouquet" in *Miscel·lània Ricard Torrents: Scientiae patriaeque impendere vitam* (Eumo Editorial, 2007), and "Lampegia" appeared in *Anuari Verdaguer*, no. 18 (2010), 148-151.

Throughout this introduction and the annotated index, scholars' remarks, several notes by Verdaguer, and other prose materials are provided in English rather than the original Catalan. The translations are my own. This English translation of *Canigó: Llegenda pirenaica del temps de la Reconquista* is based on several editions of the poem, particularly that of Llorenç Soldevila published by Proa (Barcelona, 2002), and also the original second edition (the definitive in Verdaguer's lifetime) published by Biblioteca de "Catalunya Artística" (Barcelona, 1901).

I per cert... gràcies, Teresa.

References

AARON, Daniel (1992), 'Introduction' to *The Song of Hiawatha* [1855], by Henry Wadsworth Longfellow, London, Everyman, pp. xi-xix.

BALAGUER, Víctor (1860), *Historia de Cataluña y de la Corona de Aragón*, vol. 1, Barcelona, Librería de Salvador Manero.

BOU, Enric (1991), 'Inventing the City: The Barcelona of the Poets', *Catalan Writing*, 7, pp. 16-22.

BUSH, Peter (2006), 'The writer of translations', in *The Translator as Writer*, edited by Susan Bassnett and Peter Bush, London, Continuum, pp. 23-32.

CAMPS CASALS, Núria (2013), "La recepció de Verdaguer a França: traductors i traduccions", PhD diss., Universitat de Vic.

CASASSES, Enric (2014), *Dimonis: Apunts de Jacint Verdaguer a la Casa d'Oració*, Folgueroles, Verdaguer Edicions.

CÒNSUL, Isidor (ed.) (2001), 'Estudi preliminar', in Jacint Verdaguer, *Sant Francesc*, Vic, Eumo Editorial/Societat Verdaguer, pp. 17-97.

FARRÉS, Pere (2003), Introduction to *L'Atlàntida*, in *Poemes llargs/ Teatre*, vol. 2 of *Totes les obres de Jacint Verdaguer*, edited by Joaquim Molas and Isidor Cònsul, Barcelona, Proa, pp. 67-70.

GIBBON, Edward (1825 [1776]), *The History of the Decline and Fall of the Roman Empire*, vol. 3, London, G. Love and Co. Poultry.

JUNYENT, Josep (ed.) (1994), *Manuscrits verdaguerians de revelacions, exorcismes i visions, I, Llibretes de visions de Teresa*, Barcelona, Editorial Barcino.

KOSTER, Cees (2002), 'The Translator in Between Texts: On the Textual Presence of the Translator as an Issue in the Methodology of Comparative Translation Description', in *Translation Studies: Perspectives on an Emerging Discipline*, edited by Alessandra Riccardi, Cambridge, Cambridge University Press, pp. 24-37.

LONGFELLOW, Henry Wadsworth (1988 [1860]), *Selected Poems*, edited by Lawrence Buell, London, Penguin.

PINYOL I TORRENTS, Ramon (ed.) (2002), 'Estudi preliminar', in Jacint Verdaguer, *Pàtria*, Vic, Eumo Editorial/Societat Verdaguer, pp. 23-81.

PINYOL I TORRENTS, Ramon (2007), 'Introduction' to *Selected Poems of Jacint Verdaguer: A Bilingual Edition*, edited and translated by Ronald Puppo, Chicago and London, University of Chicago Press, pp. 1-19.

PUPPO, Ronald (ed. and trans.) (2007), *Selected Poems of Jacint Verdaguer: A Bilingual Edition*, with an introduction by Ramon Pinyol i Torrents, Chicago and London, University of Chicago Press.

PUPPO, Ronald (2010), 'Making room for small-language imports: Jacint Verdaguer', *Babel: Revue Internationale de la Traduction / International Journal of Translation*, 56, 3, pp. 259-281.

PUPPO, Ronald (2012), 'Intertextual Others in Voicing Verdaguer', in *The Limits of Literary Translation: Expanding Frontiers in Iberian Languages*, edited by Javier Muñoz-Basols, Catarina Fouto, Laura Soler González, Tyler Fisher, Kassel, Edition Reichenberger, pp. 107-123.

SOBERANAS, Amadeu-J. (ed.) (2002), *Manuscrits verdaguerians de revelacions, exorcismes i visions, II, Quaderns d'exorcismes*, introduction by Joan Bada, codicological study by Joan Santanach, Barcelona, Editorial Barcino.

SOLÀ, Lluís (2013), *La paraula i el món: assaigs sobre poesia*, Barcelona, L'Avenç.

STEINER, George (1996), 'An Exact Art', in *No Passion Spent: Essays 1978-1995*, New Haven, Yale University Press, pp. 190-206.

TERRY, Arthur (2003), *A companion to Catalan literature*, Woodbridge, Tamesis.

TORRENTS, Ricard (1995), *Verdaguer: Estudis i aproximacions*, Vic, Eumo Editorial.

TORRENTS, Ricard (2003), 'Introduction' to Canigó, in *Poemes llargs/Teatre*, vol. 2 of *Totes les obres de Jacint Verdaguer*, edited by Joaquim Molas and Isidor Cònsul, Barcelona, Proa, pp. 241-245.

TORRENTS, Ricard (2004), *A la claror de Verdaguer*, Vic, Eumo Editorial.

VILARDELL DOMÈNECH, Laura (2013), "La recepció de *Canigó*, de Jacint Verdaguer, a Barcelona, València, Mallorca i Madrid (1886-1936)", PhD diss., Universitat de Vic.

MOUNT CANIGÓ

Canto I. The Gathering

Beside his brother the Count of Cerdanya,
As eagle takes an eagle for companion,
Down off Canigó comes Tallaferro one morning,
Out from the woods with his son from a hunt,
When, hearing inside the mystical chant,
He enters the holy hermitage raised to Saint Martin.

The Saint, fit out all in mail on his horse,
Inflamed with love, with a stroke of his sword
Cleaves his fine-trimmed cloak to clothe a shivering pauper;
Gentil, tender eagle, admires his armor,
And swelling with a moment's courage, utters:
"If only I were a knight like Saint Martin, father.

"Didn't I fight with you against Almansor?
Was it my back the enemy saw?
Didn't I water the ground with Saracens' blood and mine?
Why give so freely helm and shield to some,
And yet refuse them — only to your son?
Don't mothers bear warriors and paladins these times?"

"Your words give proof that you're a son of mine,
And that you're worthy of your father's line;
Now let's find out your uncle's opinion of them."
"The moment has arrived," Count Guifre agrees,
"He should make ready for the rite, and keep
The vigil through the night: come morning I'll dub him."

Like the bee buzzing inside the hive,
Gentil begins to pray inside the shrine,
Beside him the counts, and their pages and squires;
He kneels devoutly at the altar dais,
And upward at the saintly bishop gazes,
A mirror to all knights before he took the miter.

At the foot of the altar daybreak's light
Greets Gentil, dovelike in his robes of white,
Regaling in aromas of Christendom's way:
Whose wholesome counsel, for all it is wise,
Will up and flutter off like butterflies —
Alas! his fledgling heart, as well, swept far away.

"Brave thy battles for God!" the hermit cries,
"Esteem His honor more than thy own life!
Pen with thy arm, like quill, the Holy Law abroad!
Of innocence, thou ward and watch must be;
Bend not! unless to winds of clemency;
Be thou to thy people shield, to thy monarch sword!"

He sets aside the white investiture,
And piece by piece takes up his knightly gear,
The hard-ringed hauberk o'er the camisole he fits,
And on his handsome head the hood of mail,
And to his graceful torso, honed and hale,
The shield that shows Four Stripes and Sunrise brightly smithed.

Guifre, his uncle, fastens on the spurs,
Signing on his knee a cross, which he waters
With a searing tear — now the sword he raises glints
Above the altar in a sunlit ray,
As he prepares Gentil to gird the blade,
Extending forth its cross-shaped hilt for him to kiss.

Three blows of the blade on his back he strikes,
The last offence forgiven by the knight;
Meanwhile, the hermit resumes: "Thy sword is thy cross —
Rise! rise! to victory, like the Lord, with her;
Love this elegant bride with all thy heart,
Nor in life, nor death, suffer from thy side her loss!"

The chapel brims with folk all flocking in:
Elders and young maidens and young men,
For now the bell that clangs in festival has drawn them;
And with the young it seems there comes as well
Each wildflower growing bright from hill and dell,
Just to kiss the feet of the saint who smiles upon them.

Maidens have fetched and ferried in their aprons
Violets, poppies and fragrant sweet-pea blossoms,
And when they see Gentil just knighted in the temple,
They portion them out: to him and the saint,
And on his brow let fly a flowery rain,
As on the foreheads of fruit trees, the month of April.

This day all gather at the hermitage,
Dressed in their Sunday best on pilgrimage:
Peasants and plowmen, and shepherds and knights,
Each one entreats Saint Martin for a gift,
And in return, to each, he gladly gives:
For fields a good year's yield, and newborn for young brides.

The thoughts of maidens wander from their prayer,
With tempting tunes now rising on the air
From skirling bagpipes puffing green below a pine;
The piping flabiol joins in the song,
While, to the flower of maids that file along,
A rhythm struck upon the timbrel marks the time.

Linnets, their pride piqued by the symphony,
Enweave their tune within the harmony,
The turtledove entwines her melancholy cries,
The chaffinch rollicks, and the skylark thrills,
While, echo of heaven, the nightingale trills
Angelic strains learned long ago in Paradise.

Droplets mix in their trickling from the trees,
A water music tinkling through the leas,
Like pearls spread out upon a stole their notes arrayed;
Meanwhile, trembling with the wind's caress, lindens
Let go a rain of snowy golden blossoms
That maidens from Castell come cull at break of day.

Beneath an ancient arch, not far from where
The music rings and rises on the air,
From the heart of a lovely wood the Count's Spring runs;
The aspens, poplars and buckthorns it slakes
All gather close in leafy shading drapes,
And raise a bower that blocks the scorching summer sun.

The two counts repose on the mossy ground,
Together bound in melody and sound;
And there, in the shade of a maple, stands Gentil,
Who watches as the music here disbands
The dancers, there unites once more their bands,
Just like ideas, when linked by inspiration's zeal.

The lads match up with maidens everywhere,
And every pair, in turn, with graceful pair,
A necklace whose bright petals Love herself has molded;
And now, the living wheel at last complete,
In rhythm, gently, and with majesty,
Rolling to the music, sets itself in motion.

And in the midst of this harmonious wheel
There smiles the maid most lovely of them all,
With violets for a crown upon her cloudless brow.
She is no stranger to Gentil; they smile,
As on one single tree two blossoms thrive
Upon a single, loving, life-sustaining flow.

His lips now laboring quick with prayer and sighs,
The pious hermit looks with dewy eyes
Upon the scene from out the doorway of the shrine;
And newly turning to the Almighty's altar:
"Save him," says he, "O Ever-loving Father!
Let not Thy earthly daughters steal his heart from Thine."

At once the weeping, whistling flabiol
Lets fly the highest pitch its range will hold;
Just like a hive at dawn, the stir of the dance resumes;
The scale cascades with notes that leap and ring,
The dancers' feet now lift as if on wings,
And to a gladdening sun each soul lets show its bloom.

And so in splendid dance they pass the hours,
In rhythm to the tempo of the stars
That round Polaris wheel their ever-wending way;
With the cock's crow the dancers' steps turn bright,
Lifting the thick-gathered curtains of night,
And now their songs of dawn come ease the earth awake.

The links of the sardana soon undone,
A strand of pearls whose beads now lie unstrung,
Griselda, too, steps up, the rose of this bouquet;
She gracefully removes the crown that rests
Upon her head as sovereign of the fest,
And runs to give it to the knight just dubbed today.

But when she reaches him she shrinks away,
As Tallaferro shoots a look her way
In wordless grim assault: "Where do you think you're going?"
The crown she was to give falls to the ground,
And when to fetch it up Gentil stoops down,
His father thunders: "And what do you think you're doing?

"What has this shepherdess to do with you?"
"Father, she governs my heart through and through:
One day while she was berrying we chanced to meet;
The gladness in our hearts turned soon to love;
The pledge we promised then, as two in love,
If breached, word of a knight, it won't be breached by me."

"Insolence! Cast this madness out before
I'm forced to pare you down to page once more;
Would you revile these arms, your honor, your renown?"
Gentil turns pale — a solitary tree
Just struck by lightning to the quick, that sees
Its branches raining at its feet, its top uncrowned.

Griselda leans against a tree, disgraced,
And were the tears not streaming down her face,
A statue carved in marble would appear to be.
Not one takes note among the others there;
For those who dance in utter joy, what care
Is had for daisies that are crushed beneath their feet?

Bright beacon that a stretch of headland hides,
Behind the Pyrenees the sun subsides,
And here and there the twinkling eyes of stars appear;
Not so high as these, and showing less bright,
There come within the wood more stars in sight,
While Celtic chant rings out, resounding rich and clear.

These are Canigó's firespinners: they dance
On wooded slopes while hurling high their brands
Of thirty leaping flames like thirty blazing serpents;
And circling round in one immense sardana,
They pitch their sparking flares from hand to hand,
Like demons, crazed, in diabolical observance.

The twisting lights by sevens lift and fall,
And swathe in flames the nearby hills and knolls,
And through the surging smoke the forest blinks with flashing;
Rainbow rivers flitter, swell and stream,
As if between the earth and sky were seen
Firebolts and comets at war, gleaming sabers clashing.

When finally folk come back again to dance,
Before the maids have risen up, there stands
A solitary, bold jongleur among the lads,
Who launches, not without perverse delight,
Into a scornful song that's spun of spite,
And words with venom drawn from scorpions and asps.

A Saint John's Bouquet

Come listen my lads and I'll tell you a tale
     of yore,
and how it befell that on Midsummer's Day
the maids of the Pyrenees fetch a bouquet
     for their door.
There once lived a Pyrenees maiden of old,
     so it's said,
with eyes that shone blue beneath eyebrows of gold,
her face beaming bright, her each cheek like a rose
     glowing red.
A monger of flints who'd gone out for a walk,
     oh my!
came strutting his wing to her just like a hawk
to a dove: and this splinter, it seems, was now stuck
     in her eye!
On rising the morning of Midsummer's Day,
     this dove
to the river in search of some good makes her way,
and gathers up wildflowers in a bouquet
     for her love.
She takes St.-John's-wort and some scented herbs too,
     nothing more,
and twines them together so when she is through,
she's fashioned a cross she sets out in full view
     on her door.
When later that morning her lover appears
     for a visit,
he stops, as if suddenly struck by some fear —
inside, she inquires: "Nothing's the matter, dear,
     is it?"
"It's just that I can't figure out what it's for,
     sweet honey,
this frightful arrangement of flowers on your door."

"You mean you're afraid of some flowers? What for?"
     "Funny,
It's the shape I'm not keen on, like some sort of reel,
     I guess."
"It isn't a reel, it's a cross! Can't you see?
But why in the world should a cross make you feel —
     unless —"
"Yes, turtledove, some might say I was — well,
     high placed,
but then (though I hadn't quite thought you could tell),
things didn't work out as I'd planned, and I fell —
     from grace.
So now I'm in charge of alternative lifestyles
     instead.
Were it not for this posy, you'd be my new wife:
with an excellent view of the brimstony miles —
     round my bed."
And since that fine day, from the Bay of Biscay
     to the shore
stretching brightly by Roses, on Midsummer's Day
the maids of the Pyrenees fetch a bouquet
     for their door.

Hearing the tale, one white-bearded firespinner,
     Suddenly throwing his torch down in anger,
Steps up before the bard so anxious to provoke:
     With one great punch he pokes his bagpipes flat,
     Whereat, the minstrel pays him tit for tat,
And so, from tiny sprigs, upspring great groves of oaks.

Between the lads of the plains and the mountains
Lord above! the cry of war now mounts,
Till soon a louder cry renews their bond as brothers:
     "The town of Elena is under siege!
     The Saracens swarm thick upon her beach,
And fourteen galleys pour out teeming scores of others."

"We'll rise as one and rout them!" Guifre exclaims,
Now standing tall and burning like a flame,
While Tallaferro, grave, already on his horse:
     "Above Portvendres there's a place to catch them;
     Go greet these wandering lambs and we'll dispatch them
Headlong into the Tec's quick boulder-beaten course."

"And I'll go with you!" young Gentil cries out,
Now drawing up beside him on his mount.
But Tallaferro answers: "It's best you stay here;
     "You've one or two years of service to pay
     Your uncle who's christened you knight today:
Make sure he's never forced to bow by your affair."

And with these words, his father disappears;
Close beside him ride a band of firespinners
Who light the way, the swiftest and strongest among them.
     Gentil sets out with Guifre for his castle,
     His thoughts now turning to the din of battle,
The waves of vigorous limbs, the ranks of lifeless fallen.

Couriers from Cerdanya and Capcir fly
By every road far through the countryside:
They call for young and old, men mounted and on foot
To gather in Conflent — to cries of war,
The hour when dawn smiles widely on the world,
The hour when woodsmen go their way out gathering wood.

Like a quiver brimming with clattering shafts
Upon the robust bowman's back below
The tender nest of those he loves and guards
Amid the broiling, swelling battle tide,
So too this day along the Tet resounds
With sword and lance the Castle of Arrià,
Where ringing with the clang of iron there climb
Knights and infantry, packing passageways,
Great halls, chambers and archways through the castle,
While coursers in the courtyard softly neigh.
At Cornellà, inside his palace, Guifre
Waits; while here at the fore Gentil keeps watch:
For any shadow stealing through the trees,
Or firelight flashing from the sloping woods.
All sleeps inside the castle, save its troops;
All sleeps, too, along the stream, save its waters,
Where shimmering moonbeams stir in liquid play,
The brittle looking-glass of starlit skies.
All sleeps: bears berthed deep inside their dark caves,
The evening air enveloping the branches,
The lamb within its fold, and birds among
The leaves with tops tucked underneath their wings,
Stars, brightly couched on their celestial cushion,
And snowdrifts gleaming on the mountaintop
Of Canigó, as though the beaming smile
Upon the splendid sovereign of the land,
For whom the Pyrenees serve wondrous throne,
And the arching hemisphere a sparkling tiara.
The sierra seems to be a vast magnolia
Opening forth its blossoms budding white:
Gentil's soul stirs at such a marvelous sight,
And now he gazes at the glimmering scene;
His athletic squire, hailing from a shady

Slope of Canigó, discerns his heart:
"Those are no snowdrifts that you see," says he,
"They are the ermine stoles of faeries come
To dance beneath the starlit sky beside
The shores of lakes high in Cadí's bright vale;
If such a stole of finest pearls were yours,
Its worth to you, Gentil, would far exceed
Your sword, and all the science stored in books,
And all the gold and silver kept in coffers;
Should your wish be to sail, then sails you'd have;
Or were your wish to fly, you'd lift on wings.
Yet those who see that castle never leave —
Of every hundred, only one returns."
Gentil has not forgot Griselda, star
Once burning bright, high in his morning sky.
Who knows if such a portent might unite
Him with the one who pulls him from his path?
Yet how can he, the very eve of battle,
Desert the army under his command?
How can a captain leave a ship unled?
A lion leave its cubs to trace the wilds?
He turns again to watch the glistening stoles,
A trembling flame aglow upon a torch.
Who knows if they'll appear another day?
Who knows if they might be some faerie's gift,
Which if, in thanklessness, he now misprized
Might pass, like gold, into more steadfast hands?
Alas! inside Gentil's unseasoned heart
Now clash in ruthless combat love and land:
And when stern love assaults a tender heart,
Not always is it duty that endures.
And so, fast falling in that flowery snare,
He queries, feverish, "Would I be gone long?"
"If you gallop at full tilt all the way,
You should be back again by break of day."

This said, in less time than the darting beak
Of a dove takes to feed her clutch of young,
Away through kermes oak and arbutus
He flies like a shaft from Arrià's walls
Straight down to the bank of the River Tet,
Leaping in one stride its waters, and spies
The housetops of Sirac and Taurinyà
That show below like coveys of white ringdoves.
Rearward, to the left, rises Pailer Rock,
Where witches on their sabbath, after dark,
Fasten a length of spider's thread from bank
To bank, high above the River Llitera;
All those who would betray their sabbath sisters
Stumble midway, and plummet to the depths.

Up the massive base of Canigó climbs
Light as a fallow deer his fiery steed,
From roots he rises up the ample trunk,
Whose springs and torrents are its flowing sap;
Hard by the edge of cliffs and crags he rides,
Bounding the breadth of every gaping gully,
And when some hackberry hinders his flight,
He splits it through the middle with his sword.
But now the woods grow thick, where oaks entwine
With pines that thrust their pyramids out wide,
And in their midst uplifts the towering fir,
Mainmast between the mizzen and the fore.
From time to time a swath is seen to plunge
Downward off the rugged mountain summits,
As on the blackened bark of a holm oak
The withered gouge left by the thunderbolt.
It was the swirling wintry snow heaped high
On blizzard-pounded peaks that swept them clear;
An icy needle spins free from its pile,

Pitched by the wingbeat of a passing crane,
And rolls from rock to rock, swelling in size,
As militia to the sound of alarum,
And now the snowflake is a giant wave
That thrusts and rides a more powerful tide;
Pines at every turn, and beeches and oaks
Like lines of warriors marching into battle,
By hundreds tumble, swallowed in the abyss,
And nests and creatures that sheltered among them,
And herds that happen to step in their path,
Herders, too, and pastures, and crops and homes —
While woodsmen, far-off, before a sight so strange,
Fancy the peaks have taken to the plain.

In one such furrow dug where no plow cut,
Gentil now gives his foaming mount a rest;
Unable to lead him up the steep cliffs,
He leaves him here in the care of his squire,
And so, unhindered, climbs up paths of izards,
Now gripping at outcrops like a treecreeper
Up toward where the shimmering stoles lie spread,
And sheets of snow no step has ever trod.
He spies one in the center splashed with pearls,
A lily all inlaid with jeweled dewdrops;
When he reaches for it — a lovely maid,
As if sprung up from the ground, pulls it back.
"What has my gracious lady done to wrong you
That you would thieve her stole so brightly trimmed?"
"Who is this lady?"
                              "Come along and meet her,
Since you seem so keen on betraying her,
You'll see in just what garden blooms and seeds
The flower of loveliness that stirs your dreams."

In a meadow high on the mountaintop,
Gentil sees the regina and her crown,
A crown of dancing maidens weaving round her,
Engaged in mythic choreography,
With arms and feet as white as frothy waters
Frolicking with sea shells on the strand.
The fall of yellow hair of Flordeneu
Is shed in golden tangles round her shoulders,
Like sunrays in December mist when glazed
In gold by fresh frost sprinkled over fields.
Like the moon waxing in the shadowed night,
Serene and sparkling glows her countenance,
And her eyes, a pair of stars, flicker brightly,
Plucked by Canigó from cerulean vaults.
Gentil looks at her — taking what he sees
For the graceful likeness of his Griselda:
Hers is the forehead, and hers are the lips
So fit for goblet serving Love herself;
And yet her elegance recalls a queen's,
While his Griselda was a shepherdess.
In fear, in doubt, as he approaches her
He feels a flag of shame rise to his cheeks:
"Craving your pardon, most sovereign grace,
Rose of roses in this vast mountain vase,
Were it not for a maid resembling you,
My heart would now be yours to call your own."
"Gentil, are you so thankless you don't know me?
I am the flower that you recall so well,
Your heart the berry I went brambling for
The day you saw me as a berrymaid
Below, my apron brimming with the bramble,
Asleep beneath the cool and shady jasmines.
A light in the sky, for your love it was
I left the sloping azure dome of stars;
Faerie, for you alone I clipped my wings;

For you that I, a queen, set down my crown,
And let the scepter slip from out my hands;
All this, so I could clasp sweet shackles on you,
Sweet shackles tempered in the forge of love:
Bracelets of fine silver, fetters of roses.
To soar among the heavens, you'll have my dreams;
To course above the marching peaks, my coach.
From now on, you're confined to Canigó —
Olympus where we faeries reign supreme."
Gentil, held fast by unseen ties and bows,
Now follows the Faerie, who simulates
By trickery the semblance of Griselda,
Her delicate gait and her tender voice,
Her subtle smile of maiden apt to dream,
Her gracefulness of gently swaying palm,
The tangled, coiling ringlets of her hair,
Her coral lips and cheeks that show like roses:
A sovereign who, surrendering an empire,
Is slave to him whose love she steals away.

As he reaches a high ridge on the mountain,
Gentil remembers Guifre and his men.
With heavy heart, he takes a look behind;
How beautiful beneath his gaze outspreads
All Rosselló, encircled by a string
Of beacon fires ablaze on every summit!
On each and every hilltop hedging round
Ruscino's plain a watchtower rises tall,
An excellent tower that reaches the sky
To touch the star that crowns it like a jewel.
Betera's handsome head is topped with red
Just like carnations bright upon the temples
Of a maid who dances the sardana
In this most wondrous of unequal wheels.

Already they adorn the dancing watch:
Maçana, Madaloc, Coç, Cabrenç, Goa;
While Òpol, Montner, Salses and Talteüll
Raise their four flaming sconces in procession.
For never did a queen so sore at heart
Appear before her son with brighter crown,
Beseeching at his feet with teary eyes:
Don't hand me over to our foes, my son!
Gentil, who feels a sting of love for homeland,
Shakes off, for a moment, the devious dream,
And feels the blood of heroes — Tallaferro,
Oliba, Pelós — hammering through his heart;
Spurred on by its strength, he makes a retreat
While careful to avoid the siren's eye;
But ever in her ties is he held tight,
As in a spider's web the helpless fly,
And seeking his escape, on every side
He meets a steely chain of graceful arms,
And now hears words of love that cast their spell,
And turns his gaze to blue, abysmal eyes:
The sea of his shipwreck — where his Griselda,
And land and kin, are washed from memory.

At a signal from the Faerie, her maidens
Tie him fast in laces, garlands and ribbons.
"Gracious Lady," he entreats, "Set me free;
Two hundred bows await me on the plain;
If I should fail to lead them forth at dawn,
Each one will think me traitor to my land."
"It is a gentler war that you must wage —
Love's; and mark my words: Love shall win the day;
For if the chains you wear should prove unfast,
I've other chains of iron, and gold and silver."
He knows he is a prisoner, like a bird

In flight, now captive in an eagle's grip.
Gone is his serenity of soul,
Its mirror clouding to her wintry breath,
And the magical curtain of time present
Conceals from him his honor, name, and fame.
So, beside his beloved sorceress,
Carnation set beside a rose of white,
Gentil, round him a ring of flattering maids,
Into Cadí's high valley is conveyed.

That vale, today a stretch of barren waste,
Was long ago a glimmering emerald bowl
Arrayed in piney woods that gave it shade,
Trimmed with angelica and buttercup,
Self-showing in a lake that filled halfway
This monstrous goblet of Mount Canigó.
The Tarns that sparkle in that vale today
Are but the footprints of that bantam sea,
Mere fragments of that looking-glass where shone
The tall ship of the firmament in full.
Canigó extends a hand to Betera,
Tretzevents to Betera and Comalada,
And in their midst, under the blue sky's eye,
The valley unveils its maidenly breast;
A flower basket giants lift aloft,
Here poised in arms, there hoisted high on shoulders;
A wondrous garden, watered by the sweat
That crashes in cascades from off their foreheads,
And tumbles, twirls and leaps from linn to linn
As down a diving staircase crystalline,
To the vale's farthest-stretching pool of all:
A platter for an alabaster palace.
Carved in rock crystal, its towers seem to serve
As columns lifting up the azure vault,

Their enigmatic shimmer intermingling
With the timeless lamps of the starlit sky,
While, high on a hundred porphyry pillars,
Its archways are the belvedere of dawn.

Mount Canigó is an immense magnolia
That blooms on a spray of the Pyrenees;
For bees it has its faeries hovering round,
For butterflies, its eagles and its swans,
And for its calyx rise its rugged cliffs,
Silver in winter, and golden in summer,
Great goblet where the stars come drink their fragrance,
The air its crispness, and the clouds their moisture;
For stamens grow its sloping stands of pine,
For drops of dew are strewn its shimmering Tarns,
And for its pistil stands a gilded palace,
This dream of faeries lowered from the sky.

An island ever green lies on the lake,
Bouquet of flowers in a silver vase,
Fair oasis, of which the Bedouin dreams
While plying the Sahara's sandy seas.
Beeches, firs and lustrous birches give shade,
While chervil and gentian furnish a carpet,
And, in the midst of lichens, Alpine roses
Disclose the blushes coloring their cheeks.
As though of flowers, a verdant rustic footbridge
Connects the land surrounding to the isle,
Spanning the bright blue lakewaters midway —
Just like the Milky Way the starry sky.
There, on a throne of green (one cannot tell
Whether made of rhododendrons or emeralds),
The two of them sit in the spell that binds them,

Her eye set to the skies, Gentil's her face.
The scent of rosemary lifts from the wood,
Licorice lingers downward from the heights,
The sighs of lyres are heard among the trees,
From in the palace, a harp's soft lament,
From the lake the sound of the siren's song,
And the whispering of nymphs along the shore,
And ringdoves cooing in the wood nearby,
The glacier tinkling on the mountaintop,
And not far off, in caverns made of marble,
The waters trickling down their teary paths
Like strands of pearls from far-off eastern shores
Unbeaded in the crystal pools below,
And in the blue skies, timeless melodies
Of stars being born, or stars that fade away,
Planets and suns and moons that sail through space,
Fusing their lamplights in clockwork ballet,
With flowing coronas, tresses, and trains:
And the faintest flutter of wings in flight.

So, Gentil unable to break the chains
That hold the soldier far from fatherland,
Like a maidenly eye opening its lid,
The dawn now glows in its window of gold,
Sowing, garden-maid of the One on High,
Roses from her lap over the earth and sky.

CANTO III. ENCHANTMENT

Gentil, in love and fast asleep
among the trees of this delightful
isle, lies on a pily fleece
of flowering thyme and honeysuckle.

The curling vines of leafy jasmines
serve as curtains and canopy,
their starry blossoms giving fragrance
to the zephyr; to honeybees, honey.

The faeries, they too just like bees,
all hover round him when they spy him,
and marvel long at what they see —
like jewelers their most precious diamond.

One marks his eyebrows' arching grace,
one his broad forehead, still another
the smile, serene, that never fades
from his carnation lips, half-parted;

and one his silky hair now shining
golden like the dawning day,
spreading, splaying, rolling, rising —
a weave of shimmering river waves.

One dares to take his sword in hand,
and peers into its polished mirror:
a child before a burning brand,
endangering delicate fingers.

The Faerie signals to them brightly;
she has them cut his grassy bed,
and gently bear aloft the knight
in unison atop their heads.

He's led in silence to the lake
on his berth of violets and moss,
to where a gondola awaits,
elegant swan in a bath of frost.

And so a child of angels is
transported by a loving mother
upon a crib of clematis
and willow: lost in placid slumber.

Cunningly carved by Pyrenees
shepherds, the prow takes to the lake —
the Faerie's signature is seen
in its array of bright bouquets.

Decked out like April all in green,
three faeries row at either side,
their hair flung loose upon the breeze —
for if Gentil should need more ties.

When first they softly dip their oars,
all six begin to sing their song;
and from the glimmering waves they course
now lifts their sixfold siren's song.

"Dream, dream, dream," they sing,
"let fly your handsome heart!
Dream before your dream takes wing,
as bird from branch may part.

"Snow-waters lull you softly,
maidenly hearts keep watch,
your own the heart so lovely
these hovering bees would catch.

"With dreams as wings you're able
to fly your way through Eden;
meanwhile, we'll tend your cradle —
as you delight within.

"Your bed of roses made,
we'll sing you lullabies:
tunes of the lark by day,
the nightingale's by night.

"Dream, Gentil, dream," they sing,
"let fly your handsome heart!
Dream before your dream takes wing,
as bird from branch may part."

Gentil, his eyes half-open, smiles:
might this be sleep, or his heart's dream?
Love will tell, as ever, meanwhile,
his Fairie's eyes are all he sees.

He lets the boat go forth its way,
he lets love grow inside his breast:
yet sand bars lie below the waves,
and reefs to break his spirit's rest.

At times the oars fall quiet and still,
the two then smile and dream the more —
so sleeps a rock, beneath the swell,
when spent from waging watery war.

The craft slides gently over clay,
twisting a path through sandy shallows,
so too an eel may snake away
when startled by the fish hawk's claws.

As oaks grow out in boughs and branches,
so too the lake splays out wide arms,
like children roaming over orchards,
each striking out and wandering far.

Each outlet kisses willows weeping,
and crowns oases all in green,
skipping, rock to rock, like lambs leaping,
and spraying each bloom with pearly sheen.

Further on, they let fall their hair
in flowering waves that surge downstream,
as Naiads frolic free from care
in brooks by banks all crystalline.

A bright slowworm seeking its lair,
downward through the trees winds the stream,
half-pausing at a quiet pool, where
it seems a blue eye veiled in green.

Its oars drawn up like wings tucked close,
the limpid faeries' fingers let
the boat glide forward on its own:
a steed that knows the road's each step.

The vessel has a mast of silver
from which a golden sail unfurls:
it seems a darting swallow's wing
in songful flight from spring to flower.

Its lines are leafy garlandage,
which Love, that early riser, twists:
greenfinches and black partridges
alight — thinking them clematis.

The boat rollicks with them at times,
threading across a waveless sea
a shimmering wake to either shoreline —
oases unseen in the East.

At times, aground along a verge,
an arm shoves them off from the prow,
and sets them rolling from the edge,
with droves of water-nymphs in tow.

Snowy callas and morning-glories
offer them goblets of sweet fragrance,
and seem to be pure fleeting stars
fallen from early morning heavens.

Nesting among the water lilies,
the bright kingfisher wings with ease
the riverscape — a gemstone posy
tossed in play between grass and stream.

Above the water, trees bend high
in bridges and archways of foliage,
raining their blooms like butterflies
now lighting gently on their foreheads.

Mimosas drop bright yellow ones
made of gold dust from Potosí,
and pomegranates reddening buds,
in soft splashes of pebbly sheen.

The icy core of the obelisk opens
on Betera's slope cloaked in shade,
the cavern's glacier so transparent
it gives way to the light of day.

Gentil now sees the Faerie's palace,
its sunlit vaults — and here beside
the landing stage his thoughts turn less,
and less, to sunlit skies outside.

With sunset's parting kiss it gleams,
a dove half-glimpsed through leafy brake;
and lest some far-off shepherd see,
thick fog rolls all around in drapes.

A star that lights the summer night,
the palace sparkles on the lake —
a water lily sprung sky high,
to the caress of sun and spray.

For roots, like arms of faded coral,
to link the palace with the shore,
outstretch four bridges carved in crystal:
drawn from the mountain's granite core.

One leads up to Canigó's peak
with flowers that trim the path's ascent —
when walked by the Faerie, their queen,
they douse her feet in soothing scents.

Isòvol-marbled, this Alhambra,
suspended between earth and heaven,
could serve the very sun for chamber
should it stray from its western bed.

Pure arabesque is its design:
transported from the East by houris —
for pilgrims, reaching paradise,
to marvel at its wondrous beauty.

Arcades of crystal rise, stretch out,
and show in mirrored manifold
upon white capitals, set out
with palms arrayed in April's jewels.

Rows of pillars, like reeds of marble,
lift high above them icy domes,
like tree trunks raising up their branches,
filtering sky through fruits and blooms.

Below, the wide hall tinkles with
fine gold and silver tableware,
and fills with wafts of ptarmigan,
and fragrant chicory scents the air.

Not far gleam golden honeycombs
laden with honey from rosemary;
and here fresh deer's milk topped with foam
that's whiter than a frosty morning.

Peaches from Illa shine like pommels,
second to grapes from Tarascó;
by bright jujubes and sweet almonds,
scarlet arbutus berries glow.

Pomegranates and strawberries quarrel
over which more sugared rubies hold:
a fragrant fountain drowns their clamor,
and heavenly sounds pervade the hall.

Beside each table's copious horn,
maidens softly sing in choirs,
and all throughout, a harpsichord
resounds above a host of lyres.

Here birds take up the tunes of zithers:
Nature and Art clasp hands along
the trees and columns — these, together,
blend feast and forest in one song.

The monochords reply to blackbirds,
and nightingales echo the oboes:
showering notes like downpours of pearls
culled, mid-flight, by the ear of the soul.

But, for Gentil, the Faerie's heart
rings out as living lyre above
all other symphony he hears
in this, his joyous dawn of love.

Caught in the dazzle of her beauty,
he follows, defenseless, enslaved —
her eyes, skies of his soul's undoing,
where the blue of the heavens fades.

He breathes the fragrance of this rose,
inebriant perfumes of Eden —
Gentil! unhappy noble soul:
you've flung first love's doors too wide open!

The king of orbs, now growing weary,
begins to shut his westering eye,
and the beguiling queen of faeries
speaks of her love, and her desire:

"The hemisphere's soft light awaits —
let us trace our kingdom's contours,
and talk of love without restraint;
you shall judge our empire's grandeur."

And now, aside to her companions:
"Fetch me tokens of love, go hence!
search the plains, lakes, rivers and mountains,
and bring from them their finest gems;

"then to this mountain's highest peak,
when from the east the sun first rises,
and I wed the one my heart esteems,
come forth and grace him with your prizes."

A marbled gallery skirts the palace:
raised high on double rows of pillars
all in crystal strewn with bright jewels —
the tribute paid to seas by rivers.

At further ends there fork steep stairs
that meet in the garden below:
pure silver decks their banisters,
their dullest stones are white as snow.

Here, a flying chariot awaits:
to draw it, seven fallow deer;
inside, the Faerie takes the reins,
and lifts her dearest to the spheres.

Canto IV. The Pyrenees

The royal coach is made of finest gold,
Filigreed with silver, ivory and pearls;
Devised in halls of faeries to the East
By seven genies toiling seven years;
Skimming the summits of the Pyrenees,
Its wheels of seven spokes just barely brush
The grass and snow, and leave no trace below,
Just like the arc of the sun-car through the sky.

Down they glide from the alabaster palace,
And then from Pla Guillem to Verdes Pass,
And from Rojà whose arid shards are crowned
With garnet overlay — away they sweep.
Behind fade Costabona's gathering peaks,
The lofty Pyrenean ring that holds
Canigó to the cordillera like
A sparkling diamond to its golden chain.

Seeing the twosome soar along the range,
The Vale of Eina, like a garden-maiden,
Displays her skirts of brightly flowered hills
Poured out each day Cerdanya's April hails;
And they, whose ears now brim with words of love,
Pass by oblivious to your angel-song,
O seraphim! who crafted at that hour,
In Núria, the Blessed Virgin's niche.

Why lie in hiding, stream-cooled Camprodon,
Violet growing wild along your banks?
In your tenure of everlasting spring

Do you not wish your fragrance meant to please?
You and Ribes, Pyrenean shepherdess,
Who've come to the Freser to glimpse your face,
Do you not wish your grace be seen by all?
O buds, your blooms one day will be revealed.

From mount to mount by Finestrelles Pass
Up they climb to the summit of Puigmal,
And from that pitch they sight the rippling peaks
That range the wide homeland my heart esteems:
Olot and Vic, Empúries and Girona,
And in the Spanish March's very heart
Stands Montserrat, four-masted like a ship
Steaming from the East her precious Pearl.

The Pyrenees are a great tree abed,
Self-marveling how its stout branches divide
And deploy from Valencia to Roses,
Woven all the way with mounts and ranges,
Upon which float like never-fading blossoms
Homes and hamlets clustering white upon them,
And hermitages, approaching the heavens,
Seem steps that carry upward to the skies.

Passing the high headwaters of the Segre,
They reach Toses in bloom and Pla d'Anyella,
Where bees delight to find such flowers to kiss,
And lambs relish the balmy licorice;
Then Alp, an old bald head assailed by children,
Stoops, gigantic, beneath their golden coach:
A ring of timbering pines all round his peak,
Just like the tonsured top upon a monk.

The Hollow of Moixeró, green and shady,
Peering out through branches of fir and pine,
Spies them, like a pair of white partridges,
Passing by the barren crest of Cadí,
Massif where, for sole refreshment, elusive
Izards take, along with alpine lichen,
Pearl-drops that appear each day at dawn
And cooling water fresh from Fount Cristall.

Cadí's enormous cordillera stands
As a Cyclopean mountain wall thrown up
To watch and guard this earthwork of Cerdanya,
Through which the Segre carves its deepening bed.
It long ago contained a lake that stretched
Out wide, where in their fiery younger days,
These peaks would turn their gaze to contemplate
The splendor of their towering brows, now paled.

Today the lake is gone, but the range stands
As a bastion for a castle of Titans,
Erected to shield the Catalan homeland
And straddling the proud-hearted Pyrenees.
Noufonts, Carlit, Canigó and Meranges
Rise as turrets, Cyclopean in size,
Four peaks set out to stand as sentinels
Where eagles, even now, come build their nests.

Puigmal the elder, set with sturdy shoulder,
Presides as *arx* this fortress rising bold
No Saracen in seven hundred years
Has seized, each flashing spear repelled in splinters.
Not far from where Cadí meets Cadinell
The double-peaked Pedraforca looms high:

An indestructible upright fork — fit,
Should ever the need arise, for a giant.

Once they cross the Sícoris rich in gold,
Their chariot angles toward Salòria;
La Seu d'Urgell, like a page writ in glory,
Gleams amid the silky green plateau;
The River Segre, joined by the Valira,
Adorn her with their silvery vignettes,
While weaving for her garlands all in green:
Here, earth and heaven meet in symphony.

Gentil sees woods and terraces below
And past the grassy fields of La Regina,
An emerald lying shaped just like a shell,
All brimming with bright flowers and lustrous pearls:
Setúria, delectable of vales —
When sprinkled with the daybreak's early kiss,
It seems the priceless shell in which the queen
Of lovers came forth fragrant from the sea.

Now westerly the Faerie follows close
The shaded Santa Magdalena River:
Not veering from the wood, to keep Gentil
From glimpsing hermits at Sant Joan de l'Erm.
Hopping summits — Rubió to Pentina —
Below Bresca, in Collegats, she shows him
Splendorous Argenteria: whose cliffs
Once lodged a genie and his magic hands.

Curtains of pumice and embroidery,
Cascades of silver melted in midair,

Wreathes of ivy hung in rich openwork,
Celestial window shutter for a faerie,
Buds of water lilies and white roses,
As eyes of nearby maids shut fast in dream —
All sparkles bright, just like the doves who come
To nest: this garden's graceful butterflies.

Now flying close to the crags of Montsent,
She points out Gerri's splendid waterfalls;
In Cabdella, Espot and Besiberri
Constellations of lakes, azure and green:
The threefold valleys of Pallars, each mantled
Underneath their mists of vapory trains,
Appear as furrows that some giant plow
Once carved all round the triple-forked Noguera.

She shows him Boí, flower that opens out
From chaos deep within the granite core,
And in this wood of peaks weird shadows playing
Upon the Rock of the Two Spell-Struck Hunters;
Then, giving rein to her wild fallow deer,
To the top of accursed Neto she climbs,
As though, having seen the town from the streets,
To take in a better view from the rooftops.

La Maladeta

Here you have her! Behold her giant stature!
Vignemale and Ossau reach to her waist,
Puig d'Alba and La Forcada to her knee;
While at the foot of this Olympian fir,
The Alberes are but willows, Carlit a reed,
        And Canigó a sprout.

Her vast snows mother the Garona and the Éssera,
Aran, Lis, and Benasc might call her father,
Mont Blanc and Dhaulagiri, their sister:
For broader continents — a fit backbone,
For angels traveling skyward — stepping stone,
        And for Jehova — throne.

The Pyrenees are a cedar flung high;
Peoples nest, like birds, among its branches,
Whence no race-feeding vulture can remove them;
Each and every range where life takes hold
Is but a branch of this superb colossus,
        This mighty trunk of life.

Chief is she of this great army's troops,
Watchtower over this colossal wall,
Bell tower of a thousand-steepled temple,
Goliath of these ranks of Philistines
Malformed, great brow of all those breasts and arms
        In view from sea to sea.

For helm, perpetual snows catch the sun's sparkle,
For corselet there gleams her sheet of ice
Two hours in width and four or five in length;
Clouds on her back are butterflies in dance:
Dark-radiant sweep, this churning canvas claims
      The firmament for frame.

How high her plateau! How splendid her robes!
Dawn brings silver, the sun its finest gold
To keep her regal crown forever fresh;
Stars kiss her brow, then linger on as jewels,
And at times, it is said, traveling the stars,
      Seraphim stop to rest.

Catalans who reach her peaks esteem
Their land the more to see far-stretching sierras
Vassal to their own: heads bowed low before their
Titan's feet; "That giant," cry strangers sighting
Her from far away, "is a giant of Spain,
      Of Spain — and Catalan."

She sees the Ebre and the Garona, from Ocean
To Sea, and like an ageless ghost she hears their
Hymns and dirges, sees peoples come and gone,
Behind the white Moncayo, El Cid's stage,
Below Asturias's peaks — Pelayo's high throne —
      The grave where Roland lies.

Eagles cannot span her in one flight
And halt to rest, when bent on the ascent
From base to rugged Pyrenean heights;

And clouds, eager to hover round her top,
Unless the stormy wings of fire uplift them,
        Stay instead at her feet.

Often, though, they rise to restore her crown,
Wild new Sinai flashing with thunderbolts;
Blizzards lift out boulders cracked under ice,
Tossing them like clods into the abyss;
Meanwhile, the cloud, now a flaming whip,
        Claps lightning at the range.

No bird broods here, no flower blooms in spring:
Blizzards serve as birdthrong, icefields as flowers,
Flowers that open out to seal the slopes;
The dewdrops they produce are waterfalls
Which, struck with panic, leap sheer-dropping cliffs,
        Like wild and wailing beasts.

Above the ice there rise arêtes of blackened
Granite, like breakneck crests on towering waves,
Frozen seas pierced by isles of rioting rock,
Merlons of a city — poised in midair —
Like Mahomet's Bridge, perched above the clouds,
        Between the earth and sky.

Do quarrymen in winter season mount
To blast and break the granite ribs of rock?
The quarriers who climb these slopes are firebolts
That fling uprooted rocks and halve them out
To craving deep ravines and streams below,
        In thundering conversation.

With three such rocks you could build, Barcelona,
The dome and the façade your See awaits for
Crown, she herself the crown that tops your brow;
And with the sum of stones that quarry holds,
One could, should they fall, rebuild in single pieces
      Cathedrals round the world.

Slabs of broad cliffs, bones of mountains are they,
Ashlars in the wall that parts France and Spain,
Pebbles to be snatched by stocky giants
Besieged by rains of massive hailstones, should
Olympian summits witness, ever again,
      Gods and Titans warring.

What moved God to bound such beauty by chasms?
To veil in clouds the tower the heavens caress?
Why, so on earth He'd have a lookout far
From man — that lackwing angel, good or bad —
When at His feet the earth is apt to dream,
      As spouse a dream of love.

But earth still bears some distrust for her God:
Clad in rags (guise He takes to walk the world),
He called one evening at some shepherds' hut;
Nor milk nor bread nor water nor good word —
To drive him from their pen they sent their dogs
      Out growling in pursuit.

A shepherd boy, so poor he sleeps in fields,
To warm the stranger offers him his sheepskin,
And bread and fresh milk, and says: "Here, take comfort."

When at the peep of day the guest awakes,
He tells the boy: "Go fetch your goats and sheep
    And follow at my heels."

And so he did, but soon the beggar vanished;
Behind, he saw the mountain pastures empty:
The cliffs above stood out as sheep and lambs,
Rocks now formed by kids, goats, and shepherd dogs;
And their shepherds, remaining to this day,
    All turned, they too, to rock.

And since that day, when shown by local cowherds
The distant shapes that fill this dreadful scene,
The mindful traveler will cross himself;
Flowers avoid the slopes, birds give a wide berth,
Even as the summer reaper, when napping,
    Shuns the walnut's shade.

Steer clear of this place, shepherds and travelers!
Like her tales and visions, her blooms bring sorrow,
This garden of white roses cloaks a graveyard,
Beneath each marble headstone lies a pit,
The snows a sheet with which a treacherous faerie
    Designs to make your shroud.

At times in glassy caves below she sings;
Above the traveler hears her gentle music;
Beware the ear that heeds the siren's song!
The snowbridge hid beneath the glacier cracks:
The rock-cleft where he courts her in his dream,
    Is now the death-cart's groove.

Behold her sublime summit from afar,
See her face, but sleep not in her embrace;
The folds within her robes hide hideous traps.
This goddess is daughter of Neto — god
Of Celtiberians; fly! Her naked beauty
           Is the Fallen Angel's.

Yet, like wildflowers sweeping barren tombs,
Above the abyss a wondrous Angel calls:
The Angel of the birthland keeping watch
Over the Pyrenees — his vast wings span the range:
One to the headland of Cabo Higuer,
           And one to Cap de Creus.

What wrenching wails must Mother Earth have uttered
Giving birth, in younger years, to this range!
Overcome with throes by day, groans by night,
To hoist these mountains from her cratered core
Up to the clear sunlight, like waves that swell
           From deep beneath the sea!

One day, a great quake opened up her crust,
Dam through which, once cracked, burst with all its might
The seething granite's boiling river flow,
Hardening fast when ice-kissed by the winds,
And the sea, to raise it higher, hurled to its top
           Her fish and sandy deep.

Years passed, centuries piled on centuries,
Before this bone-frame of primeval giants
Dressed itself in topsoil and timberland,

Before the crags grew moss, the meadows flowers,
Before the forests filled with thronging birds,
              The thronging birds with song.

Chiseled by river and ice, the range
Took on the shape of a gigantic fern;
And when her vales lay bare like furrows plowed,
When once the flatlands stirred with life and love,
God crowned this great and mighty Sentinel's
              Topmost magnificent peak.

And Spain, long soothed by seas at either bedside
In lulling song and speech, whose headboard boasts
The Picos de Europa and Puigmal for balusters,
The Andalusian sky for cloudless canopy,
Has forward from that day for guardian had
              An Angel overhead.

See him lift his noble head through the trees:
His flowing robes seem mists; his wings of white
Mingling with the snows; corselet of ice;
His hair a sparkling light that fuses with
The sun's; meanwhile, thundering like a wild beast,
              The storm plays at his feet.

By his knee he keeps the marvelous lance
That's seen from both Iberia and France
And seems the top of some outstanding pine;
Flashing, when wielded in war to strike down
Battlements and bridges — sweeping the peaks —
              It marks the tempest's hour.

But now, each day he knits the double knot
Of amity, and bids both lands disarm:
Today's neighbors shall be tomorrow's brothers;
And drawing back these mountains like a curtain,
Glorious France and heroic, pious Spain
                Will outstretch — and join — hands.

Blinded by love, Gentil can't see the Angel;
He sees but the huge range from end to end,
Surveys the emerald earth from sea to sea,
The sapphire vault above from pole to pole,
And all the while, glistening through the mist,
The flaming golden sun-car makes its way
Downward till it dips below western waves
That blend with sky into a single girth.

Flordeneu now stirs the reins of her car,
And just to please her dearly loved Gentil,
Sweeps from Pomero in bloom to Campsaure,
Holding a course between Viella and Lis,
Dousing, meanwhile, his soul in the soft murmur
Of rivers, and of waterfalls and forests,
And in the tender song of nightingales,
And music and perfumes of paradise.

What are the Pyrenees? A malformed serpent
That, when emerging from Asturian seas
To drink the waters where Empúries bathes,
Traversed its way across a continent.
When it reached the Mediterranean Sea,
Seeing, perhaps, so fearsome a monster,

With a stroke of His magnificent sword
The Maker of all things cleaved him in two.

Between these segments, backswept by the blow,
One toward France and the other toward Castile,
La Vall d'Aran opens her flowering breast
In green, solitary, and graceful beauty.
Her fresh, bejeweled flora drawing them,
The loving pair turn often toward the vale,
But soon her elegance is lost from view,
And shades of night swell thickly all around.

By the peaks of Montoliu and Orla
They glimpse the Pla de Beret stretching wide,
A book that is made of two mountain chains
And angled on a Pyrenean bookrest;
For letters shine its sparkling drifts of snow,
And twin-rolling rivers that bid farewell,
Each bearing its wash to separate realms,
One toward the sun's cradle, the other its crypt.

The Faerie follows the restless Noguera,
Whose waters are a looking glass for stars,
Herself among them, mirrored in mid-flight
While seated just beside her youthful knight;
But soon she leaves the deepening banks below,
Skirting the pinnacles to the left,
To show Gentil the jagged cordillera
Emblazoned with the cross of Sant Vallier.

The wooded lands of Conflenç and Isil
Unfold for him green meadows, thyme and pastures,
Aubé reveals her lakes, and La Vall d'Arse
Her waterfalls: tresses of rocky summits,
Streams rebounding down the chasm's stair,
Plummeting from the clouds to the earth, where
Deep in gullies below they set to tumbling,
Combating with the spirit of the pools.

And with the warm glow of the starry host
The moon unites its scope of softened whites,
Drizzle of leaves loosed from a silvery rose
Culled by the slopes in the skirts of their vales:
The piney woods, fast asleep, wrap themselves
Inside its veil of misty gossamer,
And in the broad-bowled lake, with the moon-shimmer,
The crystalline spray of the river plays.

Tristany's three lakes are fairer for their murmur
As one pours softly down into the next;
The sparkle of Puig d'Alba and Fontargent,
The brighter for their skirts of all-year snow;
The valleys of Ordino and of Incles,
The more replete with music, dreams, and mystery
For gathering up the hemispheric shower —
Luminous wing of He who hatched the world.

Now rounding the grassy Coma d'Or, they
Course along the rivulet of Font Viva,
Holding to a branch of its verdant banks,
And climb to the top of the Carlit Mountains.
Forty lakes in tints of blue crown the summits,
Forty lakes that lie as pure as maidens;
In any one of these, in all its splendor,
Shines the night's entire array of spheres.

Beneath their winging feet they see how stars
Pass by above their heads and through the mingling
Branches of the night-dark firs: white pearls
That fly in rains across the pristine sky;
And now and then, amid the mist and starlight,
As the pair draw near a lake lying clear,
Its waters reflecting the firmament,
They think themselves on paths of stars and planets.

Just as a golden eagle soaring downward,
The golden coach descends over the Bullosa:
Elegant rubric on emerald meadows,
Cipher of silver wove in true damask;
And now those waters' snaking ribbon guides
Their fallows to the foot of Canigó,
The very spot the Faerie wants her lover,
Lest a different love now steal him away.

Shepherds, waking while they pass overhead,
And lifting eyelids half immersed in dream,
Fancy they see a pair of falling stars
For someone whom love smiles upon on earth;
Stars, watching from the upper hemisphere,
Believe they see a dove and doveling of
Impeccable feather — winging their way
To their nesting-place high in a bell tower.

Count Tallaferro rides away   on the wind,
coursing over the heights of the   Pyrenees.
When he sped from the spot of last   night's gathering,
his firespinners followed in file   behind him:
sprung from the scrublands and   sturdy of stock,
they are bound in brotherhood to   firs and oaks.
Down the Gate of Forana he comes   to Castell,
then up to Merialles and   Collet Verd,
and skirting the sierra of   Tretzevents,
at Saint William's hermitage comes   to a halt.

Inside, Saint William prays   to God,
his eyes to Heaven, his arms   a cross.
Hearing the approach, he appears   at the door:
"Count Tallaferro! There's no time   to lose —
Saracens are sacking Elna   and Ceret.
See the hard-proofed blade of   this sword:
it was Ogier's, at the siege of   Castelló;
he died in the arms of my   grandfather,
and gave him as gift this   noble sword;
it holds in its hilt relics of   Saint George.
'Entrust it,' said he, 'to none but   a warrior
who can cut through iron like sprays   on the vine.'
Take it, Tallaferro, waste   no time!"
The count does not stand by; he bids   farewell
to the elder, who raises the   grim   alarum.
The bell that tolls the alert has   little worth:
made not of brass nor bronze nor gold   nor silver,
but wrought of finest iron from   nearby mines.
No mark of the hammer is seen   on its surface:
only the prints from the hands of   the saint.
To the forge of Montferrer he went   one day:

"Bellsmiths, good bellsmiths, may God   keep you safe!
I've erected a hermitage high in   the wilderness;
its doors are of oak, its altar   of yew,
but I haven't a bell to set   in its steeple:
to sound during storms the fair-weather   prayer,
and to ring the alarm when enemies   attack.
If I settle for iron, would you call it   a gift?"
"It boils in the forge!" they mock. Take it!   It's yours!"
So the good saint plunges his hands   in the melt,
molding the mix like a potter   his clay,
and curving the flare in the form   of a miter.
He honors today that promise   he made,
tolling the tempest, and foes that   press near.

Tallaferro strikes off by straightest   of paths
down the Comalada, joining   the Tec,
and then by the quarries of green-hued   marble,
across the Virgin's Bridge, then climbs   to Cabrenç.
Its magnificent castle crowns   the hilltop,
boasting three towers all topped with   battlements;
he flanks the first two without yet   a word;
at the foot of the tallest he unlocks   his oath:
"Come down from your stronghold like God-hurled   firebolts!
The Moors are mounting thick by   Argelers;
you must fall on them now, or else   they'll rise
to pluck you falcons from your   eagle's nest!"
So said, he hears them scrambling   down stairwells:
their spears dragging, their helmets   clanking.
The count does not wait: he heads for   Costoges
now quicker than they, by way of   Sant Llorenç.
From high on a Pyrenees ridge   he sounds
his far-blasting horn: two —   or three times.
When his lips relax, in the land   all around,
farmer and farmhouse have heard   and waked:

and every town from Beget to   La Jonquera
stirs to make ready its standing   militia.
The count does not wait, there's no time   to waste:
spurring his steed, he rides at   full tilt
from high off Costoges to   Maçanet —
thrust, you would say, by the   *tramuntana*:
the hard-blasting wind off   Mount Canigó.

O mace of iron all reddened   with blood
sunk square in the ground by   Sir Roland!
If the count cannot wrest you,   no one can.
He carries a sword that's unrivaled   in worth:
its hilt made of silver, its edge   hardened steel;
when his enemies see it, they'll tremble   like grain
rustling in fields as the sickle   draws close.
O mace made of iron that once was   Sir Roland's!
Beware of the hero who wields   this blade,
emboldening his band with the Forward!   command.
Cabrera's Castle can see them   ascending:
a snaking man-forest toward   Panissars.
They pass the Trophies of Pompey,   whose head
of giants rises high above   the cork trees
to survey all Rosselló and   Empordà.
Rocabertí, half-hidden high   among cliffs,
looks on as the ranks approach   Requesens.
Here, firs and beeches, evergreens   and oaks
tangle as if lances tilted   in combat;
the count, his sword to the task,   clears a swath,
as piles of timber appear   by the path.
Had his foes seen him axing his way   through the wood,
they would scarce have awaited his   beating blows.
And now Tallaferro spots   the galleys
that fly the Crescent Moon high up   their masts
— moon of ill-omen for harvests   of homeland —

and cries with flashing eyes and arms   upstretched:
"God above! Are Moors now ministering   our harbors?"
Here, the mighty mountain bows low   its head,
like a monster stooping to drink   from the sea.
And like a storm cloud heavy with   hailstones,
plunging in lightning from high on   sheer slopes,
Tallaferro now sweeps down   off the peaks.

At the end of the range called   Puig Neulós,
stands a hill like a period closing   a sentence.
For centuries the hill shall carry   the name
of the lionlike count who sped   down its slope.
His firespinners follow, and vultures   and crows
now scenting the forthcoming mortal   remains.
"Their craws," marks the count, "will fill   with feasting."
and he speeds down a gully straight   for the harbor.
The initial assault appears   to be lucky:
the forces he falls on are not   so many,
and seem to turn tail, their galleys   and all.
He who strikes without warning   strikes twice;
but alas! this stroke goes to the   treacherous foe!
For just below Salfort there   rises up
another hill behind, that is twin   to Tallaferro's,
at the top of which stands the Tower   of Madaloc.
There, each night, the demons   gather thick;
today, the enemy too assembles   among them.
When the count first fell on them in   the harbor,
they burst out at once like a blaze   at his back,
with arrows of venom that withers   the heart.
The Christians gave battle in the grips   of death;
but few were their numbers, and soon   to be fewer:
many lie sprawled there amid   the broil;
some have been wounded, and others   lie dead.
All around them press the throngs   of foes,

unloosing their clouds of arrows   and stones;
their pitching and crashing are like   breaking waves —
of scimitars, and men living, and   men lifeless.
As the count struggles harder, his foes   press thicker;
his men, now seeing his steed stumbling,   cry out:
"The shining noonday sun   has set!
O Count Tallaferro, let God be   forgiving!"

Canigó's firespinners are flint-built   and daring,
they have battled with bears high up   in mountains;
but without Tallaferro, what more   can they do?
Bereft of head, what good are   hands and feet?
When they see him fall, they redouble   the assault:
riding down ranks of Hagar's   descendents.
The Pyrenean fir trees serve   as cedars:
parasols for cliffs, and walls   against winds;
stands of oak and pine proclaim   them kings;
their trunks fill the hollows, their foliage   the heavens;
but when from lofty clouds there falls   the mightiest,
it crushes the mushrooms and myrtle   far below.
Elbow-to-elbow, bound like a band   of brigands,
Out to the galleys the men are led   at lancepoint.
And from the ships they now hear wailing   and weeping:
The cries are of maidens, the ones   from Vernet,
who danced in the ring at the mountain   gathering.
And now, held captive just like   the men,
their tears spill out in a rankling,   bitter tide!
"Go on!! Sing!!" their jailors jeered   and mocked,
"those tunes of yours you crooned by the   River Tet!"
"Cruel captor, you'd have us sing with   hands and feet
clapped in chains? Well, here's a little   number for you:
May a bolt from the blue   toast you through!"

The count is still alive,   though struck
in the shoulder: not by any   noble blow,
but by a foul assassin's   arrow.
Yet greater than his wound now burns   his rancor:
to see his own men fall amid   their foes,
and see his men dragged off is worse   than death.
Now fourteen jailors, each one a likely   headsman,
clap him in chains like they would   a mastiff.
And rising from the ground, he utters   a sigh:
"Cursed be the arrow that injured   me only!
Oh why did its path not pierce   my heart?"
He is brought to the shore, then out   on the water.
Alas, Cotlliure, you cheerless seaboard   hamlet,
You've taken Tallaferro as   your captive,
And hold him prisoner on a Moorish   galley!
Dark are the waters, and somber   the night,
beneath low-lying cloud-murk now   gathering,
yet grimmer still must be the count's   spirit,
as now he weeps from grief — locked   in a keep.
He raises his gaze, eyes blurry   with tears:
"Help us, O Lord, in our hour   of need!
We'd sooner face death as bow to   our foes!"
And suddenly with these words he   takes heart:
and with one mighty pull bursts rope   and irons,
and to the neighboring galleys raises   the cry:
"Firespinners! Spark now! Spark for   Saint Martin!"
To his foes, sitting smug, his words   mean nothing:
those on watch in his boat give   a smirk,
and those asleep in the stern   sleep on;
but none will sleep long, if ever   they wake.
From a chip of flint there glimmers   a spark,
which touches off, in turn, a   wavering torch,
a serpent takes wing and falls on   the fleet,
and in each hull there strikes a serpent's   lair,
now whirling on criss-crossing currents   of air,

like in a pitch-black sky a rain of   meteors,
or night-sprung spirits met in   devilish dance.
The Moors, wakened by the flames that   crackle
and consume their crafts like   powder flasks,
reach for their swords — but find   them fisted
firmly by their foes above   their heads.
The waves, once black, begin to   brighten,
now turned into tombs of a   graveyard
where by hundreds and thousands the   enemy fall:
enshrined in the waters before   their time.
Meanwhile, the firespinners swim for   the shore,
a prayer on their lips, and swords in   their hands.
"Help us, O Lord, in our hour   of need!"
The Lord lends a hand: the flowering   maidens,
along with their lads, are safe   once more.

When they reach the shore the daybreak   greets them:
all gather in its glow around   their rugged
leader, whose blood still streams   unstaunched.
The bleeding has drained the count's   strength,
but his paladin's pluck will prove   enduring.
A white-bearded firespinner crosses his   pierce-wound,
and passes his fingers over   the puncture,
as if to coax out the inner   affliction;
he traces three crosses, intoning   the while:
Blow taken, blow seen, now heal,   I say,
heal in the name of the Father, Son   and Spirit.
As the shepherd heals him, the count gives   a sigh,
and turns a teary gaze toward   the mountain:
"Good count, does my cure cause   you pain?"
"Good shepherd, wounds like this one   are trifles:
I carried nineteen, and now   twenty.
My sighs are a father's — for Gentil,   not me:
O what can my son be doing   right now?"

Canto VI. Nuptials

Gentil now flies across the Tet,
riding by his Faerie's side;
his handsome figure squarely set
in the light of her hair and eyes.

Near Sirac they come to a cave:
below them, just inside the entrance,
through which they sail as on a lake,
the faeries come launder their linens.

The Basins where they scrub and lather
are of pumice, while fabrics in their
sparkling fingers seem to gather
all the gleam of gold and silver.

Each evening in the alder grove
the faeries hang the rinsed array,
which in this crystal laundry-trove
is pure as snow when fetched away.

Bright throughout with enamel sheen,
the cave's proportions wax enhanced:
its roof rising taller, it seems,
its gallery a broader expanse.

Inside, a hundred corridors
branch out like city avenues,
each strewn with lights in shimmering colors
that glaze the clay like pearls of dew.

One leads to the hall of Fullà,
and one to the cave of Bastera:
sloping down to Cornellà,
below the canal of Boera.

A soffit richly coffered crowns
the ceiling of this marbled chamber,
chisel-work of Moorish renown:
embroidery fit for the Alhambra.

The dome concaves just like the heavens,
a gilded vault in bright array;
for star-spread shine its lampions,
their glow unpaled by break of day.

The vault turns out a steady drip
of calc-spar forming stalactites,
till met by upward inching lips
Of ever-loving stalagmites.

And where the two unite as one
now alabaster columns stand,
their waxy brilliance polished on
them by celestial artists' hands.

Some resemble the trunks of palms,
topped with unrotund capitals
that fan out into lofty fronds:
arches uplifting the airy vault;

these palm trees of a haunted forest
now glow, now dim — half-dark, half-light —
when, following the nightfall's onset,
the moon turns her gaze to the site.

Others plunged in great disarray
seem to be giants battling about:
combating with torsos undraped,
or bound already in their shrouds;

The Christians and the Saracens
in every costume and proportion:
some ride on steeds untouched by reins,
like gods rising out of the ocean.

The gallery leads through to another
with new vaults opening broad and high,
where limber shadows shift and flutter
like mists that fill a windless sky.

In the distance there stands a temple,
its altar made of alabaster,
and shaped by superhuman chisel,
a starlike image in its center.

The pulpit there awaits a voice,
Its organ, hands of inspiration;
even the tabernacle enjoins,
it seems, the Almighty's visitation.

Its niche appears to be of gold,
of porphyry its splendid portal;
monks are seen in the choir hold,
and at the entrance, throngs of people.

Beyond there stretches a great cloister,
and Benedictines wandering,
absorbed in open books and prayer,
whereon their sacred chant takes wing.

Here, in a corner of the cloister,
a magnificent staircase shows:
a separate marble for each stair,
each one ingrained in white and rose.

From here their upward way now takes them
to a landing where they halt to rest:
a wondrous fountain there awaits them,
its waters splashing cool and fresh.

Should this oblivion's fountain be,
volumes of history cannot say —
but fast from Gentil's memory
fades the homeland he now betrays.

And up he climbs, higher and higher,
as if a bird from branch to branch:
above him looms a cavern brighter
than this, the one where now he stands.

And since he eagerly ascends,
each stair he scales renews his wind:
for to a heart in love each step
is but a flutter of the wing.

Then suddenly a ray of sun
shines through to sweeten his ascent,
and from the foliage sounds of song
and mossy streams in curled descent.

Here stands the Fairie's flying car,
by the entrance to the wondrous cave,
through which, as if an open door,
there pours the glow of dawning day.

And from her orient entry way,
the sun at her appointed hour
emerges in her bright array,
as if the budding of a flower.

Gentil now stands high on the summit,
upon Mount Canigó's immenseness,
before a scene of divine palette
that steals what remains of his senses.

Rosselló

"Look!" the Faerie cries, and there at his feet,
Now seen through drapes of gilded haze and flame,
Lies Rosselló in magic panorama,
As in a dream of love, he with his love,
   High on Mount Canigó.

Five rivers spring from this majestic mountain,
Five frosty rivers flow — half pearls, half ice —
Each watering Rosselló with foamy wash:
So shine in streams the loveliest of stars
   Throughout celestial gardens.

It seems a marvelous jug raised to thc pcaks
By a mountain giantess, pouring out
Five fragrant waterways from five glass spouts,
As in *pabordes*, performed on the square,
   Where dancers get a drenching.

Broad-shouldered giant, each winter giving leave
To clouds and storms and swirling snows assembling;
In every wrinkle of her splendid robes
Thrive flocks and herds on rosemary and broom,
   In every fold, a village.

Beyond Cotlliure, a vapory reddish sun
Appears from out behind the Pyrenees
Like a lantern placed on the iron-armed range —
Rising, her far-flung golden tresses serve
   The firmament for wrap.

Each day when peeping from her foamy cradle,
Her first ray crowns the king of Rosselló;
She fits him out all day in light and gemstones,
Then, dipped low behind Meranges, she sends
      The mountain one last kiss.

The bright plain expands, sparkling in the dayshine,
And rouses sweetly to the morning murmur;
The sea, asleep at her feet, dare not stir —
For fear of uncovering her dreamy daughter
      All snug in linen bedsheets.

To the left the ashy grape-rich Corberes
Rise to graft like branches on the Pyrenees,
To the right, the flowering granite Alberes;
This bow is Rosselló — two ranges bending,
      Her bowstring is the sea.

Enormous lyre upon far-stretching sands
Brimming with song some sea-god left behind;
Canigó for pommel, her wind-kissed strings
Three babbling rivers gliding through her pastures:
      The Tec, Tet, and Aglí.

"Long this vale lay hid from view," says the Faerie,
"What's grass was water: all that's green was blue;
Whales once sang where the town of Prada stands,
And Elna's cloisters cap the coral-pink
      Ivory palace of Tethys.

"Força-real and Pena were sightly isles,
Ships put in at the base of Canigó,
And by this seaboard soaring sea gulls sang
Their novel songs — where bees now hum in hives,
        Where lambs now romp and play.

"This land's the Pyrenean giant's work,
Each grain conveyed by waters from her peaks,
Rocks on the plain are bones of the range, whence
One step each century, like a worn-out guest,
        The sea makes its retreat.

"Nereids, daughters of Doris, were replaced
By graceful Naiads, issuing from urns
Of wholesome waters in Molig and Arles;
And Dryads lodged among the stands of trees
        Deep in the arks of dolmens.

"How many wars has Rosselló presided?
And — Iberia's gate — nations seen gone by?
The great range, grandstand of this amphitheater,
Has seen more peoples fight in her arena
        Than waves upon her sea.

"Phoenicians founded cities on her shores,
Yet, wandering spouse in search of other bed,
Kissed her walls one thousand years — then left;
Their gaze and tunics blue all gone from sight,
        The walls gave way to heartbreak.

"Caucoliberis and Illiberis have gone:
Their bones remain, though few recall their names.
Of Punic Ruscino, but one tower stands,
Just like a man — who all except his head —
          Lies buried in the sand.

"Beyond this column, cairn of her ruin, do you
See the budding city of Perpinyà?
It is she who has seized her queenly scepter;
I saw her born, as twig into a holm,
          As acorn into oak.

"One Pere Pinya, a son of Cerdanya,
For fear of being snowed in, spoke to the Tet:
'O take me with you to the sunlit plain!'
'Follow me,' returned the Tet — and fleeing the freeze,
          The plowman did just that.

"Taking up his oxen's traces he trailed
The coursing river into Rosselló;
When at last they reached a spot near the sea,
The river said, 'Settle here, plow and plant —
          I shall water your fields.'

"Like Romulus one day along the Tiber,
He staked a plot out with his ash wood cart;
There he set a house, field, and olive tree;
And now the house is town, broad walls the cart-tracks —
          Broad walls of Perpinyà.

"Emerging from the foam she seems enraptured,
This self-transported frothy Rosselló,
And lifting spellbound eyes to virgin snows,
She wonders which might hold more charms and treasures —
        The sea or Canigó.

"All this is mine, no queen on earth has throne
So fine: even the lowly mists kiss my feet;
This — and my heart, life, and future — I give you;
Here, level with the spheres, your crown of glory;
        Above us none but God.

"Oh! Look how my companions come in cars
Of vapory gold dust with their gifts for you:
Some slide along the slopes of grass and snow,
Filling their skirts with gems — then take delight
        In talking of our love.

"So too in royal swarms at break of day
Do bees hum swiftly off to almond blossoms.
See them ascending, how lovely and candid!
Not one less sprightly than the stars that rise
        Each night to meet the zenith."

Canigó in Blossom

A FAERIE FLYING

I see the loveliest of roses —
a rose and a carnation.
Delightful is the spring
that fetches such bouquet!
Their golden flowerpot is the mountain,
majestic vase of vases!

ANOTHER FAERIE

Let's ease up, companion:
the two are talking now.
Look, here comes Mirmanda;
what shall we do now?

THE FAERIE OF MIRMANDA

We'll circle round the summit
in a garland, and start to sing.

CHORUS OF FAERIES, CIRCLING THE SUMMIT

The heights are filled with wonder
at Canigó in blossom,
each season bright with flower —
her springtime and her autumn.

THE FAERIE OF MIRMANDA

When Barcelona was a meadow
Mirmanda was a full-blown city;
sturdy giants erected her —
and seeing them in the wood
toting rough-cut swords of stone,
great oaks began to tremble.

They raised her uttering oaths,
with rubble four palms wide,
and boulders measuring five full ells,
between the fertile fields and wetlands:
just like the city of Ripoll
midway between two waters.

That is where I lodge.
Below my home, safe behind
a slab of rock there lies a grotto:
and that is where I guard
my jewels of precious gold and silver,
as magpies hoard their brilliant baubles.

The finest piece among them
is this enchanted mirror —
who looks into it falls in love;
why, just the handle made to hold
this burnished diamond
is worth the crown of Spain.

Chorus of Faeries

The heights are filled with wonder
at Canigó in blossom,
each season bright with flower —
her springtime and her autumn.

The Faerie of Galamús

Among the vales of Rosselló
Galamús is fairest.
Bathing in broad sunshine,
she looks like mother-of-pearl,
a flower basket
lifted like a nest
high on a branch of the Corberes —
poised between the earth and sky.
Nightingales bring song,
turtledoves their coo,
and wide-winged golden eagles
provide the vale with shade.
And I, the flower of this Field,
the star that lights its sky,
can take La Fo for promenade,
for palace its enormous cave,
and for gigantic belvedere
Esquerda's summits sloping wide;
for fountain flows the River Aglí,
emerging underneath a cliff
and running off to kiss the feet
of Sant Pau de Fenolleda.
The gift I give
the river gave to me:

topaz from Bugarac,
springhead of that tendering river,
gathered on a golden thread:
a necklace fit for a queen.

CHORUS OF FAERIES

The heights are filled with wonder
at Canigó in blossom,
each season bright with flower —
her springtime and her autumn.

THE FAERIE OF RIBES

I have a gallery
stretching beneath the mountains
from the caves of Ribes
to the Hole of Sant Ou.
One end looks out on Coma Ermada,
and craggy-topped Montgrony,
the other end, the river curling
from Queralbs then down into Ripoll.
My palace stands inside a cliff
that's carved in half by the Freser,
and in the rocks on each side
I have my windows and balconies,
with ivy hung for curtaining
and honeysuckle for festoons.
Ancient oaks embrace to form
a bridge above the banks,
and those who glimpse my passing by

fancy they've seen a dove.
So here I dwell, under a spell,
daughter to Amand, Bagaudian king;
and to whomever dares to break
that spell, I promise endless treasure:
a life removed from care,
and uncompelled by death.
Meanwhile, handsome couple,
take my crown of gold.

CHORUS OF FAERIES

The heights are filled with wonder
at Canigó in blossom,
each season bright with flower —
her springtime and her autumn.

THE FAERIE OF BANYOLES

All night long I've spun beside
Banyoles Lake,
to the nightingale's descant,
and faerie song.
 My thread was of gold,
 my distaff of silver;
 the woodlands all round
 took me for the dawn.

To wind my thread
I have five wondrous winders:
the mountains of Begur,
Begur and Armenroda,
the peaks of Puig Neulós,
and Mont and Rocacorba.
The plains of Empordà
have worn no better crown,
a crown of spokes of light
all rose and lily plaited:
it seemed a brilliant peacock
fanning out his radiant wheel.
       My thread was of gold,
       my distaff of silver;
       the woodlands all round
       took me for the dawn.

Because the thread was golden,
the skeins were gilded yellow:
the sunlight's lovely locks
inlaid among the mists.
Four faeries wove this veil
deep in the Estunes,
their loom is made of crystal,
and ivory their shuttle.
Behold this veil they wove —
specially for a wedding.
       My thread was of gold,
       my distaff of silver;
       the woodlands all round
       took me for the dawn.

CHORUS OF FAERIES

The heights are filled with wonder
at Canigó in blossom,
each season bright with flower —
her springtime and her autumn.

THE FAERIE OF ROSES

What a lovely sight the sea!
How lovely on the clearest night!
She looks so long upon the sky
        her eyes show sparkling blue.

Each night the moon above
comes down together with the stars,
and in her breast that beats with love,
        she lulls them to and fro.

She learned her soothing music
from listening to infinity;
she seems the mirror of the sky,
        the sky on earth below.

Last night I saw her sleeping
there among the marshlands,
sleeping while she mingled close
        the foam among the sands.

The coral fishers of Begur
came fishing in their boats.
"Coralmen: if you take me,
        you'll make a splendid catch.

"If you must know who I am —
I'm a faerie: and my home
is Empordà; the Pyrenean
        faeries call me Mermaid."

Then, when they dove into the depths,
I surfaced with my prize:
they all came up with coral,
        and I this pearl bouquet.

CHORUS OF FAERIES

The heights are filled with wonder
at Canigó in blossom,
each season bright with flower —
her springtime and her autumn.

THE FAERIE OF FONTARGENT

From Fontargent to Orieja
I made my way this morning,
through slanting Clota Florida,
in search of wild strawberries.
and as I filled my basket,

I came upon a panner
sifting out among the sands
the precious grains of gold.
"God keep you safe, fine berrymaid."
"God keep you safe, fine fellow;
if you could part with a bit of gold,
I'd gladly give you strawberries."
"Good berrymaid, it's yours:
for berrymaids I panned the gold."
He offered me a double handful,
I only took a sprinkle, though,
and offered him the berries:
bright coral from the forest.
And as he took them,
I transformed every one —
each raspberry into carbuncle,
each strawberry into ruby.
And here you have a sample:
I've set the utmost sparkling piece
upon this ring so wide
it can divide in two:
here, if it pleases you —
receive your wedding ring.

CHORUS OF FAERIES

The heights are filled with wonder
at Canigó in blossom,
each season bright with flower —
her springtime and her autumn.

THE FAERIE OF LANÓS

From east to west I've searched
throughout my land to find
a fitting gift to give;
here: take this golden harp;
it puts all grief to rest,
and harbors only gladness.
With every pluck upon it
a voice will sing reply,
its voice, and soul, are mine.

CHORUS OF FAERIES

The heights are filled with wonder
at Canigó in blossom,
each season bright with flower —
her springtime and her autumn.

Canto VII. Disenchantment

FLORDENEU

What gift, Gentil, can I give
when my faeries bring gifts so wealthy?
What is there left to crown you with
when they've crowned you with gold already?

I shall give you my heart,
my heart and hand as spouse;
you will be my honeybee,
and I your fragrant flower.

Companions, while I slip away
and go put on my gown of green,
green as forests during May,
to greet the fest that love convenes;

while songbirds all around us sing
epithalamia in the trees,
and while the vales and hilltops bring
soft surges of their balmy breeze;

and while the sun breaks on the water,
and bathes the headland all in gold,
as on the matrimonial altar
glimmers the votive candle's glow —

tell him a tale of this — my kingdom —
my kingdom which, henceforth, is his:
tell him about my glorious throne,
my glorious throne the Pyrenees.

The Faerie of Mirmanda

The Passage of Hannibal

In the forest by Els Horts amid the oaks
and evergreens and corks, we faeries of
Mirmanda, Vallespir and Alberes danced
one day to a heavenly seven-string harp.
Suddenly there rose a din from the pass,
like a torrent roaring with heavy rains:
the clamor drew closer, the thunder rolled,
yet the Pyrenean cols sparkled clear.

Might some wind have melted her lofty snows,
dispatching racing waters to the vale?
Might herds of beasts be flying changing climes?
Or is some blizzard shaking out its mane —
battering the landscape with its blast:
flattening cabins, devouring streams and lakes,
and snapping trunks of trees as shears snip vines,
then hurling them in rolling rumbling bundles?

This storm is Hannibal's — ten thousand men
that blaze their way with mighty ax and saw,
while spanning rushing rivers in one stride;

hilltops bow their heads, valleys rise with earth,
crags and outcrops come level in their path,
trees plummet everywhere to axers' strokes:
beeches and whitebeams cut as if but cane,
and hazel trees like grass beneath the mower.

Balearians advance, armed with their slings
all wove in triple strands of pelt or hemp:
stones, when powered and fired by the whirling straps,
hum to their marks — brought down, or bored straight through.
Legions of archers follow the huge horde:
with clattering quivers carried on bare backs,
laden and brimming with poison-tipped shafts,
their flight so true they strike the wings of birds.

And further back march waves and waves of men:
waves of iron and waves of steel no end,
and no less thick upon the summit — they fill
the broad plain from Maçana to the sea.
With scales of silver glittering in the sun,
this vast and swarming serpent seems to snake from
Banyuls to Salses, as far as Osseja —
and would encircle twice all Rosselló.

Arms and armor of steel and copper shields
now flash amid the haze of dust they raise,
like lightning bolts that crackle on dark clouds
in dazzling mountain storms on summer nights.
Engines of war haul heavily behind,
as if great rocks sent rolling down the range —
the ground set rumbling to their turning wheels,
which drag beneath them boulders of Montbram.

One hundred elephants follow — like marching
peaks, great silhouettes on the Pyrenees' back:
three-hundred-year oaks bow to let them pass,
while chestnuts crack beneath their mammoth feet.
And on the highest, inside a sculpted tower,
sits Hannibal — riding the sprawling peaks.
Seeing him out of the clouds, were I not faerie,
I'd have bent my knee as before a god.

Tall, broad-shouldered, monumental in size:
a golden doublet decks his chest and waist;
he boasts the air and height of youth from Carthage,
and thunderous roar of Atlas mountain lions.
The rocky giant that commands the valley,
Great Montbram, looks small at Hannibal's feet:
seeing him, this colossus — till now unscathed
except by lightning bolt — seems to retreat.

To crown him, a hallowed legion of nobles
follows like the sun-car's radiant wake:
leather shields, broad and round, protect their bodies,
their arms and tunics plated all in gold.
Behind the nobles throng the mighty tribes
of Africa, and Spaniards with long swords:
the Romans who in Cannae see them gleam
will all but lay aside their gladii.

Along their way another wall awaits them,
whose mighty outwork is the Pyrenees:
the supreme and rugged Alpine range — topped
by yet another range of ice and snow.
Between them flows the broad moat of the Rhone:

a serpent sinking armies with one wave,
and seven mouths to swallow one and all —
their elephants, their arms, their men, their gods.

Twenty thousand horses follow: sons
of the Sahara, kin to the simoom;
shunning rein and saddle, Ethiopians
ride them, centaurlike, as one with their mounts.
Seeing them in the Alps, Italian soil will mark
what now the plain appears to tell the Pyrenees:
this man-avalanche now launched in descent
is set to crush some nation I sustain!

Atop Ruscino's walls Cerdanya's people
see their land swarm thick with battle arms;
relieved, they watch Mars' harvest waving by:
elephants, war-horses, lances and pennons.
"Rise against Hannibal!" Rome had told them.
"Rise against Hannibal!" Excellent joke!
So rise the reeds against the swelling river;
Reeds — hardly fit to stem the tide of nations.

"Make way!" now Hannibal's messengers cry,
"I go to Italy, fear not! my friends."
They lend an earnest ear, it is no joke:
"Go where you will," say those in Rosselló.
For one whole day they watched below their walls
the footmen, ballistae and chariots,
archers and crossbows and mowers and scythes —
what brings the lion of Africa to Europe?

His wish? To battle Rome's eagle: the world
for two such mighty rivals is not wide
enough; he comes to oust the world's sovereign,
and fill death's fields for Carthage or for Rome.
Why fly so quick to your death, warlike tribes?
Were not your man-streams fit to be shepherds?
In the forest by Els Horts, we faeries of
Mirmanda, Vallespir and Alberes danced.

The Faerie of Fontargent

Noguera and Garona

The vast plain of Beret
takes the form of a cradle,
with mountains for its rails
the sun peeps in like mother.
For high headboard there rises
the mountain of Crabera.
The giant cordillera
lulls its children inside.

Noguera and Garona
are its God-given offspring,
since birth they've chased each other,
have run and romped and jumped
like children at their play.
        Noguera by Alós,
                frisky,
        Garona by Aran,
                feisty.

Noguera Pallaresa
is the earlier riser;
and having viewed the north
takes a southerly course.
His brother, headed for Spain,
now sees that he's been tricked,
and left with only mountains,
while the other takes the gardens.

Like scrollwork curling back
on panels it adorns,
he veers off to the left,
rebounding off the mountains,
from Beret to Tredòs.
        Garona by Aran,
                feisty,
        Noguera by Alós,
                frisky.

While one waters wide orchards
by Bordeaux and Toulouse,
the other carries smelted silver
to Tortosa from Mount Vallier.
Here and there through dark pools,
he brightly bounds along,
till wedding with the Segre
just north of Balaguer.

Passing the plain of Esterri,
while coursing down to Gerri,
he glimpses Roland's great
iron mace, superb, half-sunk
in the grassy landscape.
      Noguera by Alós,
          frisky,
      Garona by Aran,
          feisty.

A Spaniard frenchified,
Garona, paltry patriot,
carries off to France
his wealth acquired in Spain;
and seeing us poor in springs,
spills wide into the Atlantic,
while the other, scant and salty,
trickles into the Mediterranean.

A shame the sheaf that bundled
them was tied so loosely!
Recalling other twins
that history has turned out —
paired like cat and dog.
      Garona by Aran,
          feisty,
      Noguera by Alós,
          frisky.

CHORUS OF FAERIES

Lampegia! O you who long ago
looked on her, Lanós' water-woman,
embracing in her hour of sorrow
the lifeless body of her husband,

sing, alas! her final hour,
but let your sighs and grief be heard;
your teary voice is just the lyre
that suits so well this sorry dirge.

THE FAERIE OF LANÓS

Lampegia

I

O how lovely was Lampegia!
Duke of Aquitania's daughter;
When each morning she ascended
Up the castle's topmost tower,
Those who saw her from the forest
Took her for the star of morning;
Those who saw her in the forest
The Invincible Diana.
One day Cerdanya's governor,
Abu-Nezah, chanced to see her;
She'd gone out to hunt for birds, but

It was her the Moor now hunted —
Working all his wiles to catch her,
Off he leads her, now his captive;
Useless is her golden bow, to
No avail her silver arrows,
Nor her eyes as black as berries,
These her utmost lethal weapon;
Still, I can't say which is prisoner —
Saracen or Christian maiden:
If it be the duke's fair daughter,
Thralldom never seemed so pleasing;
Rather, maybe it is he the
Prisoner; she who holds him fettered.
"You who are my heart's abductress,
Princess of all Aquitania,
What is it you wish? Perhaps that —
That my soul is what you'd ask for?"
"That belongs to God Almighty;
No, your sword is all I ask for,
Let it pierce my heart before it
Pierces that of my sweet homeland."

Abu-Nezah and the duke now
Swear a pact of peace forever,
Thanks to love, a chain of flowers
Holds together nest and branches,
Moor and Christian now united,
Languedoc and Araby, now
Blended as the day and nighttime
With a star to clasp them closely.
Chain of flowers that now unites them,
Long may God above safeguard you.

II

Learning of this, Abd ar-Rahman
Yearns to see the knot unknitted;
Crying out, "Death to the traitor!"
Off he sets for Catalonia;
Twenty thousand footmen follow,
With ten thousand more on horseback;
Leading all the throng is Zeyan,
Fearless chieftain out of Syria.
In the field he is a charger,
Flashing eel in streams and rivers,
And in combat mighty lion
Equal to his native country's.
None of this knows Abu-Nezah,
Love's embrace wrapped tightly round him;
If he sleeps, what night awaits him!
If he dreams, what grim awaking!
Near him lie his sleeping soldiers
In the fort at Júlia Llívia.
You and they, O Júlia Llívia!
See your fatal hour approaching,
Soon your foes will fall upon you,
Throwing back the fortress gate-bolts.
Her protectors prove unmanly,
Fed by fear they swiftly scatter:
Some fly toward the town of Llo and
Others off toward Angostrina.
When in woods a great oak topples,
Birds are quick to fly their nest-place.
Abu-Nezah has no escort
Close beside Duke Eudes's daughter,
Fast in flight he sees not whither,
As bereft of guide a blind man.

Now in close pursuit there follows
Zeyan with his human hound-pack;
Hearing now their yelps approaching,
Bitter tears stream from Lampegia:
"Save yourself. I wish to perish
All alone," she tells her husband.
"I'll not leave your side, Lampegia;
First I would forsake my own life."
Now they stop beside a fountain,
Now the "Font de la Regina";
They take no drink, although thirsty,
For the water would be bitter;
They take no sleep, although weary,
For the flowers seem stinging nettles.
Here is where their foes fall on them;
She leans to her husband's shelter,
Bent like basil in its plant-bed
Trodden underneath the footfall.
With his sword he shields himself and
Her behind his shielding body,
Taking on himself a rain of
Blows of cutlasses and daggers,
Till he drops upon the greensward
Stained already with his lifeblood
Dripping fast like strings of rubies
Out upon a verdant carpet.
Had not iron struck the deathblow,
Surely heartbreak would have done so:
Seeing the one he loves sequestered,
Taken prisoner by such captors,
Dove within the black kite's clutches,
Daisy snatched by shoats out grazing.
On his courser's crupper Zeyan
Takes her off to see the caliph,
To the Caliph Abd ar-Rahman,

Camped in Pyrenean foothills.
Lifting up his eyes to heaven,
In the name of God he utters —
Utters in the name of Allah:
"Eudes's daughter is delightful!
Saxifrage is she, most lovely
Of all Pyrenean flowers
At the hour of brightest blossom;
Fit for a king's coronation.
In Damascus' harem she will
Be the very queen of beauty,
Rose of roses in that garden,
Lustrous pearl upon that shoreline."
To the bitter-fated lover
Splendid was the tomb erected,
With a triangle for crown and
Dome all damascened upon it,
In the village of Planès just
Four leagues from the town of Llívia.
Those to come will wonder whether
It be mosque or mausoleum,
Whether Saracens or Christians
Were in fact the ones who built it;
Still, wherein the Moor lies resting,
Holy Mass is celebrated,
Being partly Christian he who
At the hands of Moors did perish.

CHORUS OF FAERIES

Were we now not on top of a mountain,
we'd think you were a mermaid from the sea;
but sing your mournful song no more, companion!
The story of Lampegia makes us weep.

And you, handsome Gentil, speak to us, please,
of love, since now your hour of love stands by;
as flowers speak to rivers, as shores to seas,
and seas and rivers to the tall blue sky.

The lovely harp that sleeps within your arms,
the Faerie of Lanós gave you as gift;
press it close like spouse against your heart,
and launch a song of love out on the wind.

SONG OF GENTIL

Love, where have you brought me?
Where are my friends? My kin?
Where am I?
Tell me, lovely Griselda,
        bright star of mine
        on Canigó.

Are you a lasting heaven-light?
Or just a fleeting fantasy?
Perdition or paradise?
Yet what a wondrous thing is life right here,

to see your eyes
all sparkling blue!

How could I care about the earth
while you're high on this peak with me?
See the sun come out to watch us!
Take me where he opens like a bud,
blossoming on
the firmament.

Take me where he shuts his eye,
showering gold from his chariot,
a king retiring to his palace,
and from his sun-bright gulf to starlit gulfs
we'll sail the skies
on paths of stars.

Lift me high, from branch to branch,
from where the world takes hold just like a tree,
up to the top among the golden fruit;
lift me, lift me, higher and higher —
show me the face
of the Creator.

Yet why, if you are mine, does my heart ache?
And why, if you smile, must I cry?
The universe could never fill
the sea that is the human heart;
Griselda mine,
let me cry!

And with the last of Gentil's words,
his harp trailing off with his sighs,
the sudden sound of steps alerts
the faeries — who break into flight.

Guifre has come from Arrià;
Gentil has now been gone three days:
since Saracens swept through the castle
in furious flood and savage blaze.

The Christians, their leader no more
among them, raised the cry of "Treason!"
as Moors struck Cornellà before
first warning's fear so much as seized them.

The count fought as best he could: "Run for it!"
cried shrinking warriors in the broil,
and, as if to a plague, they forfeited
city and palace and fertile soil.

From Prada to the farms and hearths
of Castell, each corner was sacked,
leaving a bare, impoverished earth,
whose head once fair its crop now lacks.

Jewels, arms, coursers, sons and daughters:
everywhere Saracens seized all,
like petals and buds torn and trodden
by a farrow amuck in garden walls.

From this unfathomed tide of strife
the count clutches what he holds dear:
Guisla, his beloved wife,
and children, fruit of loving years.

Once he has seen them safe to the upland,
watched by warriors guarding the heights,
he now sets out to save his homeland —
sacred duty of noble knights.

Up he climbs to Canigó's peak
to get a view of how things stand
in Rosselló he so esteems,
and how he might unyoke the land.

When he sees Gentil, it is now
three days he boils with bitterness —
the sword he girded on him gone,
collared like chattel round the neck.

The lad he just fit out in iron
is now with flowers and gems adorned;
a minstrel Tallaferro's son,
a Samson some Delilah's shorn.

Despite the graveness of his fault,
he seems enchanted by some fay,
for love of whom the land was lost:
Guifre is a dam about to break.

The single shove the count lets fly
sends Gentil over the precipice —
below, an agonizing cry
pierces the heart-struck emptiness.

The harp, too, bounds down jutting rocks,
scathing them with its skipping groan,
growing fainter the further off,
matching the dying bosom's moan.

The sighs and notes grow dim, then vanish,
the last of all the saddest one —
two life-breaths which, met with disaster,
now fade together on the wind.

Like a thriving, luxuriant tree
ripped by whirling winds from high cliffs,
down onto the plain of Cadí
tumbles Gentil's body — lifeless.

Flordeneu, alas! has since daybreak
been gathering fresh charms from her orchards;
like flowers in morning dew she bathed,
and like them too, diamonds adorn her.

The colors that she wears Mahomet
pictured houris wearing in dreams;
the bird of paradise, for all its
rainbowed feathering, lacks her gleam.

She views herself in the clear water
of the lake, whose surface now lies
stilled, harboring the image of her
sparkling face and smiling eyes.

Freshly fetched from nearby rose beds,
a ring of roses serves for crown;
the love that spurs her on has culled them,
brightening her face with a rose of its own.

She now steps out into her gardens,
as eager as a honeybee,
when the dimmed star drops from the heavens:
drift to drift, to rest at her feet.

His eyes are blank with snow and dust,
his face, that of a corpse; his locks,
skein of golden thread, alas! tufts
strewn yellow over scrub and rocks.

Clumped up against him press his garlands,
his silken tunic and his mantle,
his strand of pearls, the fringe and pompons
of his radiant nuptial apparel.

She falls on him, and her companions
mourn them both the length of three days,
and join with basins, cols and mountains:
"How bright the star that's gone away!"

She comes around with the third dawn,
and taking her soft curls she wipes
her tears, which soon appear again —
what use are eyes if not to cry?

She has the body laid in the bark
(what memories haunt this funeral bed!)
and with her love once more embarks,
his guide to the fields of the dead.

At either side three faeries oar,
their hearts as somber as their dress,
their hair loose on the wind no more,
falling, like teardrops, to their breasts.

They long to sing him woeful songs,
as all six faeries set to sighing,
and cannot help but think how fond
he once had been of songs of sirens.

While coursing down the streams, they pass
familiar meadows, one by one;
bright diamond from its crown detached,
she shows each one her love now gone.

The stars that see them shut their eyes,
like Flordeneu, heavy with heartsore;
and eyes of joyful birds grow wide
to hear her grieve this early hour.

The nearby jasmines once gave shade,
and showered upon him crowning blossoms
which, when kissed by the wind, they rained:
he was so graceful, young and handsome!

Forget-me-nots along the shore
see him, and ice banks moaning near,
and the sparkling crystalline source —
the clearest of all faerie mirrors.

In nearby sobbing caves of ice,
where, like pearls on shining glassware,
teardrops trickle down the sides,
the heavenly murmur sweeps the air.

Alas! in turn, each slope, each tree,
each blade of grass and starwort shows
to her, with marble heart it seems,
a scrap of his betrothal robes.

She asks them one by one for vengeance
against Guifre, and lifting high
a haze round Canigó's bright crowning
rainbow, she wipes it from the sky;

then stirs the waters of the lake
with laurel branches — drawing out
the brewing storm, with hands that raise
up cloud after thundering cloud.

Canto VIII. The Giant's Pit

Count Guifre still stands   rent with rage
high on the summit of   Mount Canigó,
between the sky and the earth,   all alone,
as now a dark fog swells on   ravens' wings,
cloaking the gardens and   the Tarns,
faerie-halls and faeries, birds   and flowers.
His eyes search outward, surveying   Rosselló,
where skies loom threatening, the land   hostile;
his gaze meets no Moors, only   the dust
their squadrons raise on roads   below.
He turns eastward to Cotlliure   harbor,
where bellying smoke now blocks   the sun.
Is it vessels or village that feed   the flames?
When he thinks of Tallaferro   he understands:
the spark he must have set to the   Saracens' galleys,
while he, alas! assaults his   sightly son!
At the thought of this his eyes   turn frenzied,
his face transmuting, as if met   with death.

Now he is struck by the weight of   his sin,
and he feels afraid, alas!   too late.
High on the vertex, like a   lightning rod,
he begs for a bolt from the clouds, but   none comes.
As if searching the dregs in a cup   for poison,
he peers in desperation into   the abyss,
a monster's dark gullet, drawing him   downward.
Will he cut short his life and fall like   a coward,
following the handsome corpse over   the edge?
Will he throw himself into the dread ravine   of Balaig?
If death is what he wishes, his foes will   oblige him:
they suffer no dearth of scimitars, no shortage   of shafts,
their lances stirring below like distant   canebrakes.

Wild and haggard, he comes down off   the summit
stumbling and blundering just like   a drunkard.
And now, above Valmanya, he blasts   his horn:
the one that his grandfather bore   into battle.
Quick to appear on the rugged   terrain
are the men of Cerdanya, and lads   of Capcir:
the birds that dispersed when the storm   first struck
Approaching Serrabona, he crosses   the streams
whose waters bathe the garden-laid   Vinçà:
oasis these ranges keep carefully   closed in,
to ward off the withering winds   of the sea.
The Aspres are the foothills branching   outward
and stretching eastward from   Mount Canigó;
and with their final swell there rises   a ridge,
recalling in shape and in name   a camel,
lying askew between the peaks   and plain.
Onto its crupper climb the assembly   of Christians
gathered by Guifre, following now   his lead.
Once their collection of lances   amassed,
down they come into Rosselló like   an avalanche,
bulking all the bigger with   their advance.
When he finds Tallaferro, both brothers   as one
are sure to smash their foes, or send   them running.

The moment Tallaferro reaches   the shore,
his archers arrive from   Besalú,
with bows on their backs and fists   full of shafts.
They mount and keep watch on   a hilltop
that's mantled in fleabane, holly   and heather,
ready to greet the men of   Mahomet,
prepared to reduce them,   or be reduced.
Moors who had moved to the fore   in a flurry
from La Salanca to the cliffs   of Queribús,
now race toward Cotlliure's   smoking harbor,

the slowest among them a blur   whizzing by.
A giant — stocky and swarthy —   leads them;
they know him by the name of   Gedhur.
When he sees the blazing ships, his   blood boils.
Bees that suddenly see the hive   on fire
swarm with speed to assault   the stoker;
so swarm the Moors to besiege   the hill.
Rising from the man-tide now are   piercing cries,
and a din of arrows dropping like   hailstones
rattling Pyrenean peaks clear   to Banyuls.
The count's bowmen draw close to form   a wall,
a wall of human flesh, and shafts   and shields;
but walls may fall if the blows   hit hard,
and blows never rained so hard as   the Moors'.
The Saracens number thirty, thirty   to every one,
and wounded, alas! the count, he who   hits hardest.
Drained at last his strength, now bent   and downcast,
his gaze roams the sky and sea   and land;
and lifting his eyes he sights something   glimmering,
a something metallic, snaking out   between mountains.
If they come to aid the giant,   God help us!
But if these be men of Christ,   God speed them!
It is not with the foes, who hold back,   that they march;
they march with Guifre, now come   to the rescue.
The men under Gedhur's command   are no cowards,
their hearts hewn sooner of oak   than elder,
the kisses once nurturing them were   the simoom's,
and they all have tangled with hyenas   and lions;
but now, caught between high walls   and blades,
before the blow can strike them, fast   and away
they slip between two armies, up   the Tec.
Up they move like smoke in   somber clouds,
passing by the shrine   of Maüt,
and through La Roca's woods below   El Portús.
If they can make their way as far   as Cerdanya,

the Segre, from there, will lead them on   to Lleida;
and there the Saracens will be   at home;
but the source of the Segre yet lies   far away!

You who in a single stride span   the Tec,
open your eye of stone, bridge   of Ceret·
you'll never see Mahomet's sons   again.
Already the Moor's Grotto watches   them pass,
heading toward the Crate, below   the Pebbles
that Roland pitched at play, while   bounding
along the Pyrenean summits,   peak to peak.
What manner of monster descends   on the Tec
from high off the crags of   Tretzevents,
snaking down the incline like   a serpent,
concealed below the grass, timber   and outcrops,
eager to gulp down men   by hundreds?
This sheer ravine that shepherds name   La Fo
is certain to swallow up riders   and beasts,
bows and bowmen, and all their   weapons,
and banners bright above the teeming   turbans.
They never so much as saw it, marching   from Reiners
up the scrubby slopes of   Montferrer.
Those who dodge it beg the wind   for wings,
the counts now close behind, like clap   after bolt,
or hammer pounding hard   on iron.
Beyond Coll d'Ares and the Tec's   headstreams,
Roca Colom stands gleaming white   as snow:
rock-dwelling doves are startled from   their nests,
pressed, just as the men,   into flight.
Soon they make their way   by Ulldeter;
none stops to slake their thirst, though   all would drink:
Christian and Moor, along with   their mounts,
but now, only a rain of arrows   beats down,
wrenching the heart like lightning   from the blue.

So let them thirst, they'll drink   soon enough,
gulping down drafts not of water,   but blood,
the blood of warring men, Moorish   and Christian.
From Count Tallaferro already   it runs
again from the wound of the   previous day.
Seeing his own blood flow, his   heart sinks:
"O Guifre, Count Guifre,   good brother!
Stop them and strike at them now,   if ever!"
The count is from Cerdanya, he knows   her roads,
her pathways of goats and trails   of izards;
he bolts up a shortcut toward   Carançà,
as if slicing away a piece of   the river.
In no time he gains on them, and cuts   them off;
while they think him behind, he blocks them   ahead:
"Surrender," he shouts, "and count yourself   pardoned."
By way of reply, the Moor   lets fly
a headlong volley of arrows   and stones.
And now the count cries, his patience   failing:
"Since you gainsay your life,   then meet your death."
He spurs his war-horse straight for   the giant,
in his right hand his lance, shield   on his arm;
they lunge at each other like ships   that meet
in stern encounter on waters   of war.
Count Tallaferro looks down   on the scene
from up on a ridge like an eagle   that's injured.
The first blows dealt are not   half-hearted,
their lances cross and crack into   splinters.
One draws his sword, the other his   scimitar:
sparks fly as the blades bite in   midair;
along with the sparks come spatters   of blood.
Shepherds, hearing the combat far   away
in Setcases and Tregurà, are hard put   to say
if the blows are those of hammers   or blades,
or the blows, thunderclap; the blades,   firebolts.
The Moorish saber resembles   a sickle,

made to harvest heads like   tall wheat.
In search of the count's, it comes   his way —
if it finds its mark, it will cleave him   in two:
his hard-ringed hauberk, his gilded   helmet,
his armor and saddle, both count   and mount.
But Guifre, gathering as much, counters   the blow,
and before his opponent can raise   his arm,
he thrusts out his sword and pierces   him through.
Like a fir when it plunges from high   off a cliff,
tumbling from crag to crag, the valley   resounds
with the rattling and quaking of   Gedhur's fall.

Since the fall of that Moor nine hundred   years past,
many an army has tramped the   shifting scree,
advancing in squalls of burning and   bloodshed;
many a bear has passed that spot, and   goats and izards,
and summers laden with storms   and hailstone,
and winters racing with torrents, snows   and avalanche,
and still, today, it is known as the   Giant's Pit.

Canto IX. The Burial

Just as the shape of a celestial
angel clad in mail appearing
to paladins of old when death's
shadow enveloped them in battle
below the Christian pennon's vigil;

so did Bishop Oliba appear
at the outset of the crucial contest
with a band of monks from Ripoll:
God's emissary never fails
at the hour of utmost urgency.

Uninstructed in war's fierce art,
Oliba knelt upon the ground,
beseeching help for Guifre who,
once having slain his great Goliath,
asks: "Whose hand was it — yours or mine?"

"Nor mine nor yours," replies the wise
abbot, his lips now naming God:
"It's God who lifts or topples men;
the slayer of foes is not the sword —
it is the Mighty Hand that guides it."

Oliba then invites the prisoners
to follow Jesus's law of living,
and take a tool and common land.
Those with wounds he treats, then declares
to each: "My brother, you are free."

At a sign from his crosier, warriors
surround with ashlars the great pit
in which the giant was laid to rest;
so done, they take the largest rock
at hand to flatten for a gravestone.

Tallaferro, not having seen
Gentil beside the grave, now asks
his brother Guifre, "Where's my son?"
and scans the armored knights and footmen
in hopes of catching sight of him.

"Gentil…my nephew," Guifre replies,
while lowering his eyes in shame,
"must still be on the mountaintop."
He tells him all about the fest,
and all he saw — except his crime.

Now Tallaferro feels a cloud
that's come to darken glory's skies
all lit by victory's brightest sun,
like Judas's shadow looming low
in sacred history's steady course.

Yet, in fear and hope, off he sets
toward Canigó beside his brothers,
eager to reach the hermitage;
nor tall blue sky nor lush green paths
deflect him from his sole intent;

nor jagged peaks nor lowly combe
where mountain springs come down to dance,
aspiring to become swift streams;
nor lakes of sparkling depths that serve
as looking-glass to stars and shepherds;

nor perfect music of the spheres,
by whose sweet chords the lowly earth
sleeps and dreams beneath the sky's wing;
nor beechy wood where Nature breeds
birds and flowers, May and April's love;

nor soothing birdsong on the air,
nor mountains draped with tunicles
of green, adorned with gleaming snowdrifts
dazzling white like starry sequins
upon their festive God-sewn gowns.

Between the counts there walks Oliba,
who leads the band that files behind,
a bright star shining through mist,
and yet, there grows within his heart
a rankling foreboding of woe.

Meanwhile, Gentil too long away,
his varlet sets out searching for him:
shepherds lead him round sheer cliffs,
he wanders through thick woods and brush,
and then hears weeping high above.

Still further up the Comalada
he comes to a pool, replenished by
the sweat from Tretzevent's lean brow;
above extends a glacial snowdrift,
that none who lives has seen unfrozen.

The vertex arches toward Betera's
cliffs — in a broad amphitheater,
vast gullet of a mighty titan:
what now is pool and ample glacier
was long ago a seething crater.

In wintertime come swirling snows
that freeze on the colossal stands
of this great jagged coliseum;
now thawed, they seem to be the apse
of a cathedral left in ruins.

Tears stream down from every rock,
and from the ice a hundred voices
rise in sinister harmony;
high crags cry out in cracking moans
and sobs, as trunks when split asunder.

Here, Flordeneu weeps with her faeries,
laying out her loved one's cold corpse,
with Canigó for mausoleum,
for gravestone snow in seven armfuls,
for lampion each night the moon.

Gentil just laid upon the ground,
the varlet spots them from a ridge,
filled with fear and crossing himself;
sick at heart, he runs to the corpse,
and seizes it from Flordeneu.

She cries out, and with her companions
she vanishes like mist in mountains,
which raise the echo of her grief:
for those who sorrow in their midst,
the rugged peaks, too, have a heart.

The grieved varlet speeds his beloved
burden down through woods and breakneck
paths, till he comes to Sant Martí,
the two counts and Oliba there
when now he lays him on the greensward.

As a beech struck by lightning bolt,
Tallaferro drops to the ground;
the corpse he holds sends chills straight through
his heart — for all his twenty wounds,
this blow has struck him to the soul.

He soon comes to, and hot with rage,
shoots blazing glances all around him,
and roars out loud: "Who killed my son?"
Guifre, now backing toward the shrine,
half-dazed, but loyal, blurts: "I did!"

Like lightning Tallaferro draws
his flashing sword meant for his heart,
but quick to thwart his grim design,
Oliba gives Count Guifre a shove, then
throws the door — and himself — between.

A deer that feels the piercing shaft,
the murderer falls at his feet
and tells of his horrible crime:
his life, alas! he takes for lost,
but as Christian, would save his soul.

Like a sledge on the log it splits,
fists pound against the ancient door,
which groans and cracks under the hammer;
the wood gives with the first blow, but its
hinges and stanchions are of iron.

The count lets fly his pounding might
against the door that stands half gaping:
so the smith's hammer on the anvil;
the shrine resounds like pealing bells
sent reeling to their mighty clappers.

Square on the spot that cracks the loudest,
he hurls his whole titanic body,
bursting now through hinges and bolt.
The door collapses with a quake,
the entrance now an open gate.

Bent, in his wrathful resolve,
on profaning the sacred shrine,
the count seeks out his brother's bosom,
but then hears *Ego te absolvo*,
and lets the sword fall from his hand.

"As God forgives, forgive me too,
or deal to me the death I dealt,"
says Guifre kneeling at his feet.
"Crush me, or let the deathly worm
feed on my heart, long as I live."

So disarmed, that monster of war
falls to his knees beside Count Guifre,
before the bright cross of the Savior,
then both hearts lock in fast embrace,
fresh miracle, Jesus, of Thy love.

Oliba, too, weeps with compassion,
more tears to quell the fire of wrath,
more ash to bury the burning spirit;
the three flames of this pyre unite
in single prayer throughout the night.

And so their gentle prayer takes flight,
lifting to God on flaming wings,
three spirits bound in single love;
so, too, three tender dewdrops gather
inside the calyx of the flower.

At the first ray of light that strikes
the eyelid of the shrine's great window,
the bishop says Mass for Gentil;
their hearts now shine with light renewed,
like altars bathed in April's glow.

Enacting the High Sacrifice
to show unbroken brotherhood,
he offers them the consecrated
Gift of God, angelic wafer,
each happy brother taking half.

Saint Galdric on a nearby peak,
digging out his hermit's grave,
now wets the earth with woeful tears.
Recalling fair Gentil he marks:
"How brief is the life of a flower."

Behind the high Byzantine cross
the mourners file among the trees;
Gentil lies on a bier of lances —
a newly blossomed lemon balm
crushed beneath a careless beast.

Ahead of the corpse walks Oliba,
leading the somber cortege
in his great black cope; and his grief,
more poignant with each step he takes,
punctuates the sorrowful chant.

The party of mourners comprises
the elder monks and knights in armor;
beside the Count's Spring, tears well up
from all, but none like Tallaferrro's —
who gives Gentil one final kiss.

Maples and hackberries, too, sigh:
to look upon the life now spent,
of all the laurels that most graceful,
with bright blue eyes that gleamed with joy,
but gaze no more, and now bring tears;

to see the vital sap and hue
now vanished from a thriving palm
that swayed when kissed by gentle breezes:
bright flower of Besalú that faded
the hour it opened to the sun.

The bell, too, sighs with men and trees,
like a sister mourns a lost brother,
to whom just yesterday she sang
the moment that he took the sword,
and now lies fallen like a tree.

Deep inside the canyon wolves howl,
the wind whistles, whirling through pines,
dismantling May's regalia,
the sky puts on its darkest cloud,
and tears stream from its tall blue eye.

Drop by drop the Count's Spring flows,
concealed in leafy undergrowth,
like a faerie having a cry;
though nightingales may sing, each note
is but a moan that aches the heart.

The Cadí surges down its course,
stirring, as if pebbles, or bones
in a reliquary, great boulders.
And if the sky seems like a shroud,
the earth, too, seems a vast cadaver.

They lay him lengthwise in the grave;
interring last his handsome head
once sprinkled with a faerie's kisses;
the bishop raises up his crosier:
"All in this world is vanity;

"beauty, pleasure, dreams of glory,
the names history learns, then forgets,
and crowns and scepters, gold and silver —
all effaced beneath the gravestone,
all swept by winds into oblivion.

"But part of man eludes the tomb:
the chrysalis remains behind,
while he ascends into the light;
so the gladiolus's rich fragrance,
its petals plucked by winds, lifts skyward.

"There we shall see Gentil again
one day — just now my chalice raised
for him, I saw his spirit rise,
his gaze upon the Blood that cleanses
hearts of all their earthly sorrow."

The gravedigger fulfills his office;
how bitter Tallaferro's grief
to see his greatest treasure buried!
He stands, dour and desolate, like
a victim led to sacrifice.

Count Guifre, kneeling on the ground,
still clutching the lad now half buried,
begs him forgiveness for his sin.
The other knights, their lances upright,
look on as Gentil disappears.

Oliba alone stays serene
of soul, so they might bear their pain;
at times he has them look toward heaven —
harbor of suffering souls, where
flowers have no thorns, hearts no heartache.

"I'll stay with him up on the mountain,"
Guifre resolves. "He need not lie
alone on such a rugged bed.
My soul and his are fellows now,
and mine shall sleep beside his grave.

"My son Ramon will run my house;
Here, I shall build a monastery
to end my life in penitence;
since I failed in the science of living,
I'll try to be better at dying."

Oliba answers: "Should a cloister
stand upon this shady slope,
graft it from the tree of Cuixà,
which like the sky that strews the night
with stars, has sown the earth with saints.

"If I can recall it to mind,
I will tell you the long-lost tale,
and show you the roots of this tree
which, sprung from tears and yet unfamed,
raised a saintly harvest to heaven."

Eixalada

"To Aquae Grani
one day where Charlemagne,
        that sun of history
in the noonday of his glory,
        sat on a throne of gold,
the flower of dukes and princes
        of all peoples
bowing low their noble heads,
        five elder monks

meagerly clad in coarse habits
      took themselves,
and beset with sighs, spoke these words:

    " 'Beloved King,
whom God gave to the world
      to increase His Kingdom,
less famed for scepter and crown
      than greatness of heart,
hear, if you please, our cause.
      In Eixalada,
not far from the Llívia-Prada road,
      we monks till now
kept a shrine and monastery,
      a thriving garden,
ancient parchments dear to our hearts,
      and choir books
we gleaned more eagerly than gold,
      altars of marble,
cloisters ponderous and bold
      where rough chisels
had hewn the beasts that roam
      the woods nearby;
we kept an ample hospice
      where paupers
took shelter from cold and hunger.
      But disaster struck!
And now no trace remains:
      in a trice
the racing river's tide
      erased it all,
as though it never was.

" 'On sunlit slopes
in sight of La Tor of Cerdanya,
       lived d'Enveig the Knight,
too quick to procure his pleasure.
       His joyless wife,
jealous of his fatuous love,
       prayed to God
that He might bring her husband home,
       who since the day
he chanced to spy her bathing
       in the lake,
like a water lily in bloom,
       he grew too fond
of the fay of Lake Lanós.
       He fell into those arms,
and fast caught up in fetters,
       promptly forgot
his children, wife and hearth.
       Like a silver ribbon
that tethers to the plain the thankless
       range of Puigpedrós,
the River Tet frolics as it flows
       down from Lanós
to kiss the monastery left
       a rack and ruin.
At times as far as Capcir
       the knight follows
the hectic river coursing clear
       in cruel hunt
of drakes graced with painted wings,
       black-and-yellow billed,
that when lifting into radiant flight,
       more than fowls,
seem skysome jewels
       of finest gems

crafted by sylphs and water sprites.
      Our prior happened
to come across him with his lover,
      and offered
friendly counsel: 'Hear me well,
      you cannot forsake
your wedded wife
      for a fay!'
Having heard enough, his lover
      stamped her feet,
and swore by all the gods of the East
      to put an end
to these monastics and their monastery,
      and at one blow
to crush both nest and clutch.

      " 'Before Planès
in the wide basin of Barrès
      there stretched a lake,
mirror to the king of spheres by day,
      blossom-strewn
looking-glass of stars and moon
      by night.
La Llacuna remembers well enough,
      noble village
sitting humbly on its rock
      beside the lake,
like a slumbering fishermaid
      who next day
wakes to find nor fish nor lake.
      Inflamed, the faerie
speaks: 'I shall be the floodwaters' gate:
      this very night
the bedspread of cloisters and chapels

will be the lake,
and hive, honey and honeybees,
    when they awake,
will reel and tumble to the sea.'
    So said, she leads
the tide by day's last light
        into the valley,
where the Tet, like a horse
        galloping its way,
halts at the barrier of rocks
        piled up by God
when He raised the Pyrenees.
    One thousand years
of waters eroded the sands,
        abrading
the chain's locking links,
        and of that range
a mere earthwork remains.
    Into the crest
the knight now delves his spade,
        dislodging the rocks;
with each stroke the thick wall
        thins and wanes.
Not even a giant stands so many blows.
    From the dam
a spring comes gushing out,
        soon a river,
that swelling broader and taller
        is soon a sea
enveloping towns and fields.

" 'For Eixalada
the final night has fallen!
            In the monastery
we had just settled into sleep,
            when a crashing
roused us from our slumber.
            We leapt from our beds
and raced half-dressed to the choir below.
            The chapel lay deep
in a nest of darkness, like an eye
            with lid drawn tight.
Then, to heighten our horror,
            by the dim glow
of a single fading lamp we saw
            the shade of Ogier
come out from its ossuary and signal
            toward the door,
which opened with a mighty blow of mace.
            Five only —
we five flew close behind the shade
            out from the shrine,
struck with terror, seeking safety
            up the mountain.

" 'When the shade vanished before us,
            we looked behind:
alas! the monastery was no more;
            the roaring tide
had swept it up and sent it tumbling
            down the slope:
the monks, the chapel, the turrets,
            altars and marble,
flocks, crops, columns and trees.
            A single cry

rang out from the night's core
      coupling with thunder,
rolling the length of far-stretched lands
      and sowing,
more than fear and anguish,
      swift death.

" 'Farewell my fine fellowship
      of paradise,
books, companions, happy cell,
      fair altar,
mystical cell of the One on High.
      Sweet monastery,
if only I had joined you in death
      at that hour,
to spare me the sight of daybreak
      spreading its light
again on the graveyard of our beloved!

      " 'Then we came upon
their remains, clothed in their cowls
      amid the sorry muddle,
along with the corpse of d'Enveig,
      pierced through
with the tool of his foul handiwork.
      Following the Tet,
in the vale of Codalet so dear
      to our hearts,
like a precious gem the sea tosses
      on the shore,
we lit upon the likeness
      of Saint Michael,
like a star that shone in our sky

laden with clouds.
It alone we salvaged from
the deluge!
You who govern the world from Erin
to Mount Vesuvius,
erect for us a cloister where we may,
night and day,
accompany the Archangel.'

"The Emperor,
even as he dries his tears,
makes his reply:
'Servants of God, His hand has saved
you from the grim
tempest that has taken your ship.
Henceforth you shall have
a cloister and a shrine on the plateau
by Cuixà,
since it was that spot for sojourn
chosen by
Saint Michael's wondrous likeness
from Eixalada.
Just like the bird her brood,
he officers
from high in heaven my armada.'

"The monastery
soon sprang up and bloomed,
like an olive tree
along the banks of the Litron.
Sky above Cuixà,
studded with so many stars
by Abbot Garí,

and Peter Orseolo, Marinus
       the saintly ascetic,
and Romuald the anchorite!
       Rosselló
has not seen since such constellation
       of spheres so glorious
as in the noonday of her history

       "With such a seedbed
to set the world teeming with saints,
       if you plant
your cloister, then that psaltery
       will surely fill
these canyons to the brim with soothing hymns."
       Count Guifre replied:
"Then to this end let us act at once!
       And to ensure
my vow propitiates my nephew,
       near his tomb
I shall dig my own as well,
       So I may lie
as servant at his master's feet."

Count Guifre makes his way to Cornellà
To see the countess and tell her good-bye;
How cheerless seems to be the landscape now
Where all in sunny love was once so bright!
The passing trees appear to nod and rumor,
As if their parley touched upon his crime,
And gleeful birds that flit and leap about
Appear resolved to keep him at a distance
And tell each other of his murderous act —
No easy tale to tell on tongues of harps.
The gaily colored greenfinch trills no more,
The nightingale no longer sings, but moans;
For from these harps the joy has now been drained,
Only the chord of agony remains.
The drowsy wind that dozed within the wood
Stirs abruptly, like a wild beast disturbed;
Chilling howls are heard in the ravine,
The screech of barn owls high on roofs, and thunder
Rolling closer, low from cloud to cloud,
The sky's portentous prelude to the tempest.
Approaching now the palace of his forebears,
He sees his graceful Guisla at the window,
Framed by matching vases of carnations
Set out to brighten up her windowsill;
He pictures her in mourning like a widow
And lowers to the ground his eyes in shame.
Each step upon the stairway he ascends
He waters with a bitter burning tear;
And on the topmost it is she who weeps —
Her head a lovely willow's hanging low.
The words that they exchange are laden with
The utmost heartrending, sorrowful grief:
"Farewell," says he, "my wedded spouse in life;

To tear myself from your heart is to break
My own afflicted heart, as if a limb
Some cruel arm has ripped out from its trunk."
"I'll never let you go," replies his wife,
"I'll never let you leave, your life is mine.
Did you not promise everlasting love
The day we took our vows before the altar?"
"And I will always love you, just as ever,
But it must be, alas! from a monk's cell
Inside a cloister to be raised above
The shrine of Sant Martí del Canigó.
There I should have left this life, on the gallows,
Between the earth and sky, devoured by crows;
Through God's compassion I am granted life,
To Him I mean to render its remainder!"
His wife, heartbroken, searches for reply,
But with the anguish welling in her soul,
Her eyes alone now brim with bitter tears —
Speechless, she finds no utterance but a sigh.
He stamps a final kiss upon her forehead,
Embraces her, and now, about to leave her,
He turns to her with tearful eyes himself,
An infant snatched away from mother's breast.
A sob now rises from the bottom stair,
And from the hall above is heard a cry;
Nearby the count there weep the knights and pages,
Nearby the countess, ladies of the palace;
With Guifre's exit, she sees the entrance of
The chilling specter of her widowhood,
Her hair drawn low to cover up her face,
A dark mantilla trailing at her back,
Her arms a blossoming magnolia's fallen,
Torn by the tempest even as it thrives,
And her sloe-colored eyes and iris forehead
Now clouded over in a haze of sorrow.

When once again her heart comes round to her
And grief's initial tide subsides, she sets
Her mind to bringing to the shrine of her
Unwedding, some goodly stone of her own.
Out to the palace yard she makes her way
With a needle made of silver, and thread
Of silk, to embroider a simple altar cloth
Of richest fabric made of finest weave.
Upon it she depicts the Catalan Stripes,
And scatters here and there a star among them,
As if the dreams that came to her from heaven
Were interlaced with dreams of her fair land;
She makes her signature below the emblem,
And places at its top her countess-crown.
With each and every stitch of her bright needle
She lifts her eyes up to the rising cloister,
Now letting fall a tear to be inset
As if a pearl upon her handiwork.
Her maids would gladly give her some diversion,
As soon her thoughts close tight upon her troubles,
Her mind upon her inmost memories,
Like ivy pressing round a ruined palace.
Everything speaks to her of Guifre: the mountains
Where he battled wild beasts, the spring where they
Once rendezvoused, and which her palms would cull
And offer him in tender cupping hands,
The verdant landscapes where they gathered flowers,
The brook upon whose bank so fresh they sat
And watched the flowing waters at their feet
Serene just like the season of their youth,
The willow where they once found shady rest,
The pine trees whistling up the mountain pass
Like shuddering strings upon a psaltery
When strummed on by the rudely bred mistral.
The birdsong now heard faint and far away,

Mysterious sounds that reach her from the trees,
The muttering of the wind among the leaves,
Seem mounting waves upon a sea of woe.

All at once she hears a maiden singing,
As if a gull whose song far out at sea
Has come to ease the edges of the waves
With some elusive streak of cheerfulness.
As Guisla hears the melody she thinks
Its strains too joyful for her sorry state.
"Who can this angel-maiden be," she wonders,
"Whose merry song resounds, while others sob?
I'll pay a visit to this maid: perhaps
She has some remedy to soothe my grief."
From porch to garden, from garden to wood,
She shoulders her sheaf of measureless care,
And sees how every flower droops like her,
She who was, just yesterday, their queen;
And now the more she hears the wondrous song
Pour from the trees, the more distressed she feels.
Up the archway bends the curling vine,
Bejeweling it with golden grapes and pearls,
And up the elm tree climbs the clinging bine,
With wifely arms that clasp her wedded spouse,
And close among its branches calls the ringdove,
Softly speaking to his mate while fetching
Blades of grass he gathers for their nest,
Within their wispy hearth enormous rafters.
The brook busies itself courting the nymphs,
Marguerites smile up at the golden orb,
Each boasting on her breast its golden double,
Divine seal of hearts ever true in love;
Yet never was the sky so thick with clouds,
And never was the earth so steeped in sorrow;

O landscapes of Conflent, how you have changed!
What heartache now you visit on your mistress!

Like a traveler beset with thirst
Who hears the murmur of a limpid brook,
Into the wood she ventures, toward the maid
Whose song rings clear among the pasturing flocks,
And who upon a stump of oak now sits
And through her distaff draws her woolen thread.
Moved to delight by such richness of song,
Once near the spot, she now approaches softly,
So soft her footfall does not crush the clover,
Nor does her passing even bend the grass.
Very close she hears her now, quite nearby,
Between them standing cool and brambly shrubs;
Drawing aside the osiers and clematis,
She glimpses the maiden through rosebush shoots:
She seems a wild rose, unfolding her petals
Far from gardens, beneath the sun and starlight.
The skirt she wears is woven of coarse fabric
And matches in its hue her olive hood,
Her espadrilles are white and well for walking,
Of finest hemp just like the thread she spins.
The song she sings is one that tells of hope
To see once more the one for whom she longs;
Away to war against the Moors he went,
Now that his colors come home, so must he.
With each new stanza of her tender song
Guisla lets go a melancholy sigh,
As one by one she relishes each note —
Dewdrops sprinkling cheer on her sad heart.
Now looking up, the angelic shepherdess
Wonders at the troubled lady, and moved
To compassion, she calls to her companions:

"What's happened? Can some thorn have pierced her foot?"
"A thorn has pierced my heart," replies the countess;
"You sing so sweet and I am racked with grief,
I, who am the Countess of Cerdanya,
The princess of this Pyrenean precinct.
Can you have come upon within these woods
The fount of joy that cures the sad of heart?"
"Indeed, I happened on it one spring day,
A skysome day my soul will not forget;
But alas! it came to pass that soon
My heartache dimmed that sparkle once so pure."
"Who is this lad you love?" inquires the countess.
"He is the flower of lads that grace these banks;
Fair angel among knights who serve the count.
Unknown to you alone — who are his aunt?"
"Gentil?" utters the countess, seized with dread.
"Gentil!" sighs the maid by way of reply;
And the poor wife of he who bore the blame
Now drops as if struck by a deadly bolt,
Her lips of carmine turned to chilling frost,
Each rosy cheek now blanched a white musk rose.

Her handmaids carry her off in their arms
Toward the palace she left that erring hour,
Like a living cadaver toward the tomb,
Whence she sees, above, the tomb of her love.
Conflent, her farmsteads and her towns now weep,
And lone turtledoves in their nests now weep,
And low skies, where the tempest breaks, are like
The eyes of Guisla, a fountain of grief.
But fair Griselda has no tears to cry
When, simple at heart, it all comes to her;
She has no tears to cry because in life
The cruelest storms set in completely dry;

And so, unable to pour out her pain,
She muddies her head of flowering years
And forfeits all sense — so lovely a star
That fades into a falling night of madness.

Canto XI. Oliba

Settling now into their sacred task,
The warriors leave their swords for builders' tools,
They set aside their spears and take up mattocks,
And in the mountains where below a gravestone
Lies fair Gentil at his eternal rest,
There stirs an army now immersed in labor.

Have you seen how ants race to and fro
On stubble fields in summer when the sun
Turns grain to gold and prods its ears to open?
One takes hold of a grain, another hoists it,
This one pushes, that one pulls along,
Till all the grain is stored, the chaff repulsed.

Such is how these men toil: where one stakes off
Uneven ground, another works it flat,
Or digs a trench to bed foundations down;
Pines and firs are felled by timbermen,
Then sawyers square them off, and in such fashion
Stonemasons sculpture the marble and granite.

By noon the structure hangs one foot of stone
Out over the sheer-dropping precipice,
Whetting the pangs of the eager abyss,
While, the other foot firm on solid rock,
It spreads and rises on the craggy heights,
A child come forth to match a giant's growth.

As to the bugle's blast a light brigade,
The cloister's columns fall into formation,
Each capped with rustic capital for crown,
Where — at the sculptor's voice — comes to a standstill
(There among the leaves of palm and agave)
A veritable throng of beasts and birds.

Beneath the earth the Blessed Virgin's Church
Gives primitive support: though blind and dark,
This new celestial orb provides fresh light.
The fervent flame of prayer long since lit,
Another temple stands on top — a golden
Statue on a silver pedestal.

Granitic columns of natural grace
Upraise upon their fronts their triple vaults:
Ancient sign of the highmost Trinity;
And seeing her there so fair and maidenly,
Like a giant that guards a maid from danger,
A bell tower takes up vigil by her side.

Sturdy and wide, colossal in height,
Commanding the two valleys and the combe,
And still it rises, story laid on story.
As both a belfry and a tower of war,
It stands as the earth's titanic attempt
To draw a step closer to paradise.

Its cells are truly cells of honeybees,
Built small and fine within this heavenly hive,
For honey joy and gentleness abound;

And for the twenty monks who settle in,
It's to be found in prayer, and in the shrine,
In flowers of the earth, and in the flowers of heaven.

Sowing the length of the psaltery's strings,
They crown their monastery with a garden,
And when they step outside the temple, incense
Mingles with the lavender's aroma,
And both lift upward in a single mist
To the vast altar of the peaks and spheres.

Amid this chaos of rioting rock,
The monastery rises like a specter
Within the very throat of the abyss;
It is a flower sown by whirling winds,
And if for water heaven sends its dewdrops,
For heaven will it flower throughout the centuries.

Guifre runs his eye along his work
Like poets their most lofty inspiration,
Crowned with light and streaming radiance
When soaring high above the peopled lands,
Star whose aureole, beaming bright and clear,
Will light upon and grace its author's brow.

That selfsame star, alas! will be a thorn
For he who planted this divine of flowers.
His cell looks out on waters from Cadí
Trailing through the southerly ravine,
And seem to him to murmur night and day:
"O Guifre! I saw your murderous deed."

The roaring waterfall of Les Esqueres,
With tresses flowing loose amid the greenscape,
Iridescent in the glimmering dawn,
Reminds him of another head of hair
He once saw hurtling down off Canigó,
Tracing its golden hue upon the snow.

The current seems to tell the rolling pebbles
Of his crime, the pebbles tell the rushes,
Whose hollow stems inform the world's four winds,
And now the world itself vents its rebuke:
"Oh why, why did you cut short Gentil's life?
Where have his gentle grace and love gone now?"

A grim phantom visits him in his torment,
Urging him over the edge of the gorge,
And others, below, lift their ceaseless cry:
"Come quick," they shout, "for you belong to us,
What you think the roof is taller than you know,
Beneath these depths there lies the wailing hell-pit."

Seized with dread he now abandons the cell,
And takes a smaller one facing the north,
Closer to the temple's sheltering core;
Then God, seeing him turn to prayer and the cilice,
As if with His hands, lifts him from his anguish,
Granting him again his restful days.

Alas! his wound one day reopens when
He hears of the storied life of Saint William:
How when he built his church in Vallespir

The shepherds and farmers came to his aid,
And in repay, to those who wished it so,
He went about blessing their flocks and fields.

One day, weary of carrying a great
Ashlar, one of his workmen cursed the rock;
So the hermit spoke: "Throw away that stone!
It is unfit to raise my temple's walls;
A single fleuron flawed will taint a crown:
Fling it far, or take it back where you found it!"

"And so I am myself that cursed stone
Within the House of God I have erected,"
Declares the count-become-monk with a sigh.
"Sinners are not fit to live with saints,
The raven and the swan are poorly paired,
Nor is coal, for diamonds, a proper peer."

Taking a chipping hammer, near the chapel,
Just between it and the grave of Gentil,
He sets to hollowing out his last retreat.
The rock is rugged, the labor hard-going,
No tool of iron or steel is he himself,
And yet his deed outstrips both iron and steel.

Guifre does not give up; day in, day out,
He meets the surging rock defiantly,
A week, a month, and still another month,
The tougher and harder the blue slate grows,
The tougher the mighty hand of the monk,
Hammering the harder, no matter the angle.

One day arriving from his bishopric,
His crosier in hand, miter on his head,
Oliba finds him chipping the raw rock:
"What is this labor of your sturdy hand?"
"I open up a window," he replies,
"To see more often to the other world."

Window or hollow, the work is soon done,
And like the weary quarryman inside
His quarry, he beds there when evening comes
And sleepiness weighs heavy on his lids;
So, by the languid glimmer of the stars,
He lies there every night as though a corpse.

In his dreams he sees the moon rise up,
A lampion in a temple's dusky nave,
Where winds and rivers are the thundering organ.
He thinks himself dead, on his catafalque,
With glowing candles strewn like stars all round,
And listening to the mighty *Dies Irae.*

His grave is the enormous mountainside,
For barrow rise steep skies of crystalline
Each point whereon he wanders in his dreams,
At the soles of the Being the world pays worship,
Seeking, among the many gone before,
The soul of young Gentil he loves so much.

When from high above his dream descends,
It lights, like a bird, on another grave
To look on what was body of that soul,

And his aching martyrdom is soothed
As he sees the solitary tomb-angel
Embrace them both beneath his sheltering wing.

Often to his bleak and bitter cell
There comes the awful calling of Griselda,
Who in her madness cries: "Gentil, Gentil!"
Then, her golden hair tossing in the wind,
She knocks, with snowy hand, upon his grave,
Where April will no more bring forth a flower.

At times, no longer hoping for reply,
She breaks into a run along the slope,
Rousing the cloistered count with her shouts:
"Beneath which tree can my loved one be sleeping?"
Then: "Good monk, do not worry if I cry;
So many days now I have searched for him!"

Meanwhile, Oliba examines the temple:
No nook escapes him; for now in Ripoll
He founds another monastery still,
Inspecting for this reason now these stone
Branchworks, and the moldings and the foliage
Carved to fetch kisses from the gentle west wind.

To that place he transports all in thought,
From the tip of the vane to garden benches,
Transmuting, combining and supplementing,
And thus his fantasy unfolds a work
That, before sprung forth to light of day,
Sprouts and bears a trunk and branches — then blossoms.

He sees it all: his handiwork in marble
Is like the lofty tree lodged in the nut,
The marvelous flower within the tiny seed;
He sees it whole — except the frontispiece
To set as crown upon the edifice,
To give the golden form a wondrous face.

To this the loving artist turns his dreams
Each night, set down by day in drawings then
Consigned to flames when seen again the next,
And with his mind now bent upon the dream,
He turns his back on other projects soon
Forgotten, as a rock beneath the sea.

One day at the hour of rest from work he calls
The monks out to the yard beneath the trees:
Three days now he has plied from dawn to dusk,
Sketching, writing and wiping with his staff,
Like at the seashore waves upon the sand,
When cradled softly by a gentle breeze.

"Look!" says he, and before them they can see
The portal that his genius has conceived,
The sacred history of the Holy Faith,
Written here in stone by the hand of Rome,
With the crosier of a bishop for pen,
And for paper, a slope of Canigó.

Seven mysterious cantos has the poem,
Seven fleurons will deck the diadem
To crown Santa Maria de Ripoll;

Seven heavens of beauty pure and divine,
The Bible stamped on Catalonia's heart,
The present, past, and future of the world.

The first page of this work of dedication
Represents Eternal Glory on high:
The Lamb of God upon His starry throne
Holds out the book of life for all to see,
And speaks these words unto the race redeemed:
"Ungrateful men, take heed how much I loved you!"

The four Evangelists behold the book,
Mysterious creatures who turn to look
With wings that spread just like the wings of birds,
And, nearby, four-and-twenty white-haired elders
Sing: "It is fitting that the One Most High
Unlock the golden Book of Seven Seals."

There follow peoples of all tribes and tongues
In vast procession come to pay Him homage,
Patriarchs, apostles and confessors;
Virgins hold the lily of purity,
Martyrs the palm of their martyrdom,
And, beneath their arms, doctors bear their books.

In his chariot of fire is seen Elijah,
And, in other stories and prophecies,
Moses, Jonah, David and Solomon;
The Red Sea is crossed by the Israelites,
Who struggle with the cruel Amalekites,
And the Ark of the Covenant rounds Jericho's walls.

In glory the zither and psaltery,
The fipple flute, the tender violin,
All hail the victory of Jesus Christ;
The prophet king, amid vassals and nobles,
Seems to say: "Praise Him peoples everywhere,
Sky, seas, and lands: together let us praise Him."

Oliba shows them all in great detail
This mystic garland fortifying faith,
He points out here Saint Peter, there Saint Paul,
Who stand as solid pillars of the Church,
Propping up the sky with all its spheres;
One holding fast the sword, the other the key.

Within the band of the arch they both upbear,
Their lives in twelve *ex votos* are depicted,
Joined high at the feet of the Holy Lamb;
When during life they walked upon the earth,
Brave in savage war with vice and error,
Already, then, their souls had joined in Him.

At His feet, refuse of the dark abyss,
There lies the fierce dragon of heathenism;
A pair of eagles descend to the earth
To combat the confusion of its wrath,
And while one with his talons grips it tight,
The other with his beak puts out its eyes.

He shows them now two lions met in battle,
Pitching in fury at one another;
A fleeing centaur flings an arrow at them,

But man, whose passions have apportioned him
The figure of a monster, from this chain
Of things impure extracts himself too late.

Commanding now his steed the ready rider,
At last become the master of his passions,
Full clad in all the trappings of a knight,
Approaches the ferocious animals,
Who when they see him aim his piercing lance,
Bow down in tame submission at his feet.

Below it all, he sees Lucifer's fall
From heaven, and Adam's fall from paradise,
And stretched upon a floor of endless flame
The damned, these new Laocoöns with their limbs
Entangled in the diabolic coils
Of slithering apocalyptic hell-brutes.

The fiery phrases of the architect
Impel the mighty project into motion,
Monsters and saints, songsters and men-at-arms;
The pairs of eyes and lips in stone now open,
The bows of violins begin to move,
And music flows in streams from the façade.

Now Christendom will have its arch of triumph,
Once broken Mohammedanism's yoke —
Catalonia's arch to Jesus Christ.
All those who pass through that arcade can say
That they have seen in sacred synthesis
The world, the temporal, and eternity.

Count Pelós, the first of Barcelona,
What pantheon to your renown, what crown!
No worldly king had ever better headstone.
But alas! the wise bishop cannot know
That even while he raises it, death visits
The limbs of his own illustrious tree.

Count Tallaferro, not so long ago,
Set out to make a journey to Bellcaire;
His wish was that his son Guillem now take
For wife a maiden hailing from Provence,
Known to her brothers by the name Adela,
And to young troubadours, Flor de Poncem.

So while Oliba recounted the epic,
There came to them a messenger in mourning
Who with his message brought them heavy grief:
Said he: "Count Tallaferro, he is dead!
All Provence falls into mourning for him,
The very heavens seem to burst with tears.

"One evening he set out to cross the Rhone
When suddenly the racing waters swelled,
Beneath his high-strung horse the ground gave out,
And when he spurred it, suddenly it reared
And turned so sharply as to throw its rider,
Then both were carried headlong down the river.

"Searching and reaching for his struggling steed,
The weight of his armor pulling him under,
He floundered and gasped, and grappled with death.

An hour went by, and on that fatal bank,
In the shade of a willow's greeny tresses,
My deceased seigneur slept his final sleep."

Praying to the Almighty for his soul,
Oliba, heartsore, set out for Ripoll;
Returning to the cloister of Conflent,
He finds his only brother in this world
Has fallen sick, stricken with a grave illness,
A teary star upon a sparkling sky.

"God keep you," says Guifre, "like Tallaferro
I soon will leave behind this earthly exile.
If only now my heart were clean like his!
This very night beside my sepulcher
Saint Benedict, our patriarch, struck thrice
With his foreboding mace to let me know.

"Cell and cloisters, farewell heaven on earth,
Harbor of peace upon this sea of war;
Farewell brothers I loved with all my heart:
Hold me, as yourselves in mine, in your memory;
I go now to await you in His Glory,
Beside the fountain of eternal love.

"And now that greedy death has come for me,
I ask you one more thing, a final favor:
Plant the Cross of Canigó at the summit;
That with its loving arms raised up to God,
It may uplift the gaze and steps of all,
And from this mountain wipe away my crime."

"So shall we all monks of this land go forth,"
Replies Oliba, "And the sign of the cross
Will stand on the mountaintop like a temple;
And flocks of angels will turn out with psalms
The warbling that infests this faeries' dovecote,
And they will lay to it their rightly claim."

Canto XII. The Cross of Canigó

Chorus of Monks, below the mountain

Before death takes the count,
let us make the ascent to Canigó's summit,
and with the sacred sign of victory
crown the brow of Rosselló.
        The cloud-murk,
vast shroud of some perished giant,
        now covers the heights,
putting out the stars one by one;
but the cross that guides us rises even higher.
        Onward, in God's name, to the top!

Chorus of Faeries, at the top

Along the clouds and mountainsides
the thunder rolls like a hurtling chariot;
somewhere nearby strange voices rise,
        while ours grow weaker.
Who comes to desecrate our palace?
        Must our swarm take flight,
handing over honeycombs and hives?
Fall on them, tumbling tempest,
        O bellowing cloud!
Unsheathe your blade of lightning!

CHORUS OF MONKS

Like a furious volcano, the storm
has stirred up Canigó's summit;
snowdrifts rise in revolt, breaking loose
under the blizzard's beating wing,
        raising a thundering
of chargers bolting in the chase.
Woodlands are sheared like vines at pruning season,
great boulders are plucked from their perches,
        sent rolling and careening
amid the quake, and forests vexed to fury
        wonder whether Canigó,
with its tops of snow and roots of marble,
        has been clipped from
the Pyrenees like a twig from a tree.
        Still, the cross guides us:
        not a hair from a one
of our company's heads will fall;
        no leaf so much as budges
        unless it is His will.
        Onward, in God's name, to the top!

CHORUS OF FAERIES

Away with you, hermits and monastics!
No palace glimmers in the sun like this one;
though you would turn it into shrines and cloisters
        for your doings with angels,
it pleases Flordeneu to keep it.
        But alas! our mountain
is besieged like a fortress scaled
        by foes from seven sides,

to the sound of holy hymns and chants
and pealing of a hundred bells.
Let's fly from this place! Our palace crumbles,
its crystalline columns are cracking,
Alas! just like the snow that crowned our mountains,
our thawing glory carries far downstream!

Chorus of Monks

We can see through the scattering fog
how Catalonia now looks greater,
        seen while scaling
the terraced shoulders of this giant mount.
        For crown the daybreak's
snowy skein brings silvery rays
        that slowly turn to gold.
        The morning star
        sends its last kiss,
fading in the sparkling mist,
like a diamond veiled in golden hair.
        O salve! Catalonia,
        the dark night lifts,
        the clouds move off,
and like an excellent enormous crown,
the sun now tops your clear bright brow.

The Faerie of Mirmanda

Good-bye, Celtic city of Mirmanda,
        I leave you now for good;
you never will again see faeries

dancing in rings across the river
     the month of May.
You'll watch your houses fall, one by one,
as the river, too, dwindles away.
And weary of standing guard over ruins
     your mighty oaks,
     long spared by lightning,
     will lie down to rest,
and your palaces and towers and pools
     will lie like flowers and thorns
all scattered over fields that time has mowed.
     A thousand years you'll be
a quarry for these towns: from your double walls
will be erected many a castle and abbey,
your noble altar stones will serve as tables,
     your menhirs, boundary markers.

THE MONKS OF THE MONASTERY OF EL CAMP

The Saracens once driven from Provence,
Charlemagne one day beset them
     at the foot of Canigó,
     his army led, as once
God's people by the ark of the covenant,
by Holy Mary's likeness wrought in bronze.
Stricken to the very blood with thirst,
his sword falls from his swarthy hands.
     But Charlemagne understands:
he drops to his knees before his Patroness,
and sinks into a fertile field his Joyous,
     whence fresh water flows,
     renewing their strength
     to repel from the heights

the foes of their sweet homeland and their God.
In everlasting memory of this feat
our cloister at El Camp was founded;
And so the Star of Tuïr was to be,
        Star of its glory,
the Blessed Mother, our Lady of Victory.

THE FAERIE OF GALAMÚS

Flower-strewn valleys of Fenolledes,
farewell; farewell, you wilds of Galamús;
        and from your wooded lands,
        too, washed by cooling waters,
disciples of Christ have driven me!
        Good-bye, lakes of Noedes,
Black Lake, Blue Lake, Star Lake —
        mirrors of these piney woods
below an immaculate sapphire sky!
        How cheerless now you seem,
after all your freshness and your sparkle!

THE HERMIT OF GALAMÚS

        I can see you from here,
        soothing hermitage,
        I yearn for you
        like the tiny bird
        its nest among the foliage.
        In the grotto yesterday
I came upon Saint Anthony's divine likeness:
        in sign of victory,

he held the devil, depicted as a piglet,
at his feet. Did an angel of glory bring it
to ease the harshness of the wilderness?
        Fair Thebaid of mine,
        vestibule of paradise,
in you, together with this seraph,
        fair Thebaid of mine,
        I'll have a happy death!

The Faerie of Ribes

        Good-bye, caves of Ribes,
        I shall not see you again,
fountainhead of healing waters,
        flower basket of Núria,
her bands of greenery spread against the skies.
No longer will the carters hear my song
climbing their way along the paths,
nor will shepherds at their morning watch
        in woods catch sight of
my linens hung along the riverbank.
        Never more will knights
aflame with love come to the cave
        that only love could open;
        if someone chances on my nest,
        they'll find it sans myself!
To these valleys Count Arnau soon comes
        decked out in fire and flames
        to take my place of fame;
woods, sunlit slopes, farmsteads of my heart,
        Farewell forevermore!

OLIBA

If Count Arnau is to come, so will others,
    with the cross in their hands
and the love of Christ in their hearts,
to set the earth alight with fire divine,
and make of it a flaring orb of love.
The heavenly troop set out from Monegals
    when already the surge of
    Saracens was receding,
and where the Ter and the Freser touch waters,
    the spot where Ripoll was born,
they raised their abbey on that tender isle —
Catalonia's foremost bulwark.
These angels of the homeland there kept safe
    her history and her treasure;
they cradled there her nascent spirit,
and lulled her with the songs of ancients.

THE FAERIE OF FONTARGENT

    I'll not be seeing you again,
    Andorran timberlands,
rivers of Fontalba, lakes of Fontargent;
    Alas! my Catalan mountains,
I cannot tell you *a reveure*,
as I see you fading, fading to the west!

THE HERMIT OF MERITXELL

None too soon this faerie's flown the nest!
        These valleys boast
a finer queen and lady — in Meritxell.
Making music at her feet, the Valira
flows, melodious, from Ordino to Soldeu,
and takes the form of a gigantic lyre,
        its arms crystalline.
        On her forehead gleam
twelve tarns, the Pessons, bright crown
adorned with sparkling jewels passed on
as gifts by peaks that hoist the heavens:
Ariadne's splendorous crown,
        detached from the zenith,
looming high between the earth and sky.

THE FAERIES OF ROSES AND BANYOLES

Farewell, towns and beaches and forests
        of these ungenial regions.
What seemed like dawn of our glory has fled
        on wings of fleeting dreams,
like passing meteors streaking the skies
with vanishing trails of glowing silver;
so, too, there rise and fall, beside the sea,
        the sand hills of Begur.

THE MONKS OF BANYOLES

When Charlemagne set Girona free,
two armies appeared in the open:
each met in battle with the other, like woodcutters
swinging axes deep in canyons;
the rain of blood gave new baptism;
amid the horrid storm a flash of lightning
signed a fiery cross upon its ivory head.
For their revenge the Saracens engaged
        a dragon from the dark abyss
that swallowed maids and children,
and any knight who dared to fight the beast,
and with him, too, his horse, armor and pennon.
Savage, monstrous, misshapen,
it muddied the lake with its venom,
and thrashed the waters with its bulking tail,
heaving waves upon the town.
        When at last Saint Emery the Monk,
answering the call of orphans and widows,
        came forth from his cloister,
the bloodcurdling monster fell at his feet.

THE MONKS OF SANT PERE DE RODA

When the flaming sword of Chosroes
burned the holy city of David,
on its eternal, invincible throne
the city of the Capitoline trembled.
Under swift sail Pope Boniface placed
the head of the Prince of Apostles —
        token entrusted to you,
O Catalonia, my sweet land!

With loving hands the sea
conveys her cargo toward the Pyrenees,
to the foot of the cape, once throne to Venus,
     now harbored by the cross.
Below the holy cross the mariners
     encase their treasure
     of saintly relics.
When the iris of peace sparkles anew
     they return, the tabernacle
     now wreathed in greenery.
Covering the spot are cloaks of ivy,
and bine and clematis adorn the draping
that in celestial May the angels brought to bloom.
Seeing that Saint Peter took a leafy nook
     for his reliquary,
     they raised a chapel,
which blossomed, like a flower from the bud,
into a cloister — Sant Pere de Roda.

The Faerie of Lanós

Farewell, soil of Cerdanya,
my one day paradise!
Alas! how sorely I will miss you,
     for on your sunny slopes,
     bright garden of my love,
I saw my dreams bloom forth!

The Provosts of Núria and Font-Romeu

The sound of crying comes
    not far from Font-Romeu and Núria:
it is the flock of faeries that our gentle
    song has frightened.
Let us sing, as their somber night declines
    in the rays of your aurora,
    O Morning Star
    of Núria and Font-Romeu!
    Be thou Regina
    of our Pyrenees!

Chorus of Faeries

Let us fly, Flordeneu: leaf by leaf
your crown of gold now falls away;
the flight of our illusions scatters
like butterflies in buffeting winds.
Let us leave these sovereign summits,
and to some far-off island in the sea,
from where, centuries since, we surely came,
the memory of Catalonia in our hearts,
        go to end our days.

Flordeneu

Years ago, this very day, this very hour,
        I sat here with Gentil;
        the dawn's kisses
hovered on his brow, like honeybees

hovering near the brows
of buds that April opens with his breath.
        And from this peak today,
where his footsteps lie imprinted,
        to all my heart has loved
        I now must take my leave!
        The heights are filled with wonder
        at Canigó in blossom:
        that's how it was here once
        for me — it is no more.

Faeries, departing

When leaf-letting November draws near,
        swallows gather
along the shore to make their crossing;
and so our flight takes us, too, far from you,
        sweet Catalonia, as
we cast one longing teary look behind.
        One day the swallows will come back
along with lilies and poppies, and loves,
along with songs of lads and maids:
but as for us, you'll see us nevermore!

Chorus of Monks

We've made it to the mountaintop,
        Pyrenean balcony;
from here we now see France and Spain:
        we shall unite them with the cross.
                        (*As they plant and praise the cross*)

Golgotha's blossoming tree upon the rock,
O cross! Open heaven's passage with your crown,
and shut hell's entrance fast below your trunk,
and with your outstretched arms rebind the world.

Oliba

The glimmering band of a full-colored rainbow
bends tall above the Cross of Canigó,
celestial crowning brushstroke of an angel.

A Child

    Like pearls in the sand
left by the blue rolling waves,
I see among the clouds, in skies
now turning clear, saints and virgins shining.

Chorus of Saints among the clouds

    Crux fidelis, inter omnes
    Arbor una nobilis.

Abbot Garí

O sweet school of Jesus's love
I planted in the cloister of Cuixà!

Its gentle fragrance rises
        finer than a garden's;
see how white the stoles of those disciples,
and see how love divine streams from their hearts.

CHORUS OF SAINTS

Silva talem nulla profert
Fronde, flore, germine.

SAINT ROMUALD AND SAINT MARINUS

Like a nest of nightingales among wild roses,
        I see our hermitage
before the monastery of Sant Miquel;
        divine apparitions
        descended to these woods,
and from them lifted up our souls to heaven.

SAINT ORSEOLO

One day, as mighty doge of Venice,
I gave the sea my spouse some golden rings;
        for Thee, sweet Lord,
for Thee I kept my soul and heart.
As if God-sent on angels' wings,
        Into your company
        I came to live, Garí,
        at the abbey of Sant Miquel,

and left behind my children, wife and kingdom —
parted with all this, for this piece of heaven.
    Often until daybreak
a divine ectasy took hold of me;
one morning when the stroke of matins
summoned me to the choir, the door was shut;
    I called to be let in,
but no-one heard: no-one, but the Lord.
He sent me down two loving angels
    who brought a golden ladder.
    Happy, oh! happy
are they who climb, O cross! your thriving
    branches: tree of life,
    which bears for us the fruit of heaven;
to rise to Glory's boundless joy,
    thou art the golden ladder!

CHORUS OF SAINTS

Flecte ramos, arbor alta.

SAINT VINCENT

Lower thy branches, O cross! to Cotlliure.

SAINT WILLIAM OF COMBRET

Shelter the villages of Vallespir,
flowery nest I made my restful home.

SAINT NARCISSUS

Keep safe the walls of immortal Girona.

SAINT EULÀRIA

Take thy place on the shield of Barcelona.

SAINT LUCIAN AND SAINT MARCIAN

And on the heart of our mother Ausona,
that she may flower in science and piety.

SAINT DAMASUS

And in Empordà, Rosselló and Cerdanya,
          in Catalonia and in Spain,
let the faith of Jesus Christ live again,
and let Mahomet recede at His feet.

OLIBA

          Do you hear?
The bell of our monastery tolls;
and with it, my heart, too, asks you to pray
          for my brother who now lies dying.

Chorus of Monks, Kneeling

Proficiscere, anima christiana.

Released from the bonds of the body,
the immortal chrysalis breaks with the world.
Receive him as spouse in Thy arms:
deliver him, O God! from the vortex of hell,
as Lot from Sodom in flames,
Daniel from the lion's jaws,
Saint Peter and Saint Paul from the chains
    of bloodstained Rome,
    Job from a sea of afflictions,
and Moses from Pharaoh giving chase.

A Child

In a dawn that glows serene and pure
    I see him rising up,
    his youth restored, and free:
    two among the righteous
sail downward with a smile to greet him.
One boasts a noble warrior's build,
resembling the figure rising from exile,
    who now embraces both,
and one looks like an apple tree in April.

CHORUS OF MONKS

The first must surely be Count Tallaferro,
      the other, fair Gentil.

OLIBA

Glory to the Lord! The clouds of sorrow
enshrouding for so long my soul
are scattered like the clouds that filled the sky;
      the night recoils
      repulsed by light of day
now shining through the eastern window.
      Our beloved land,
long held beneath Mahomet's yoke,
      like a well-armed warrior
drives back the Saracens toward western lands.
Count Berenguer of Barcelona
      broadens his crown.
Catalonia wakes with legs astraddle:
one this side, one flung over the Pyrenees,
like an Amazon astride her courser
      drifting into sleep
just having left some demigod's embrace.
Catalonia seems to be a golden eagle
      who with each wing commands
one side of this enormous mountain range.
Now vanquished the titanic Almansor,
of Islamism once the evening star,
who may tell if some outstanding hero,
one of ours, will raise his measureless sword

of mighty conqueror?
Who may tell if, judging small
his home and crown, he might take up that sword
and trace the boundaries of a sweeping realm?

CHORUS OF NOBLEMEN

We set off to the thunder of war,
like a storm decending from the peaks;
    let us drive out forevermore
this cloud of locusts from our fields;
    later we shall plow them:
    our halberds we shall turn to plowshares,
our swords we shall recast as sickles.
Today the Paynim is the grain to harvest!

FINAL CHORUS

Praise to the Lord! The land we love awakes;
how tall she stands, rising vigorous from sleep!
Look what a buttress the Pyrenees make,
her brow in the sky, the sea round her feet.

She waves the powerful lance in her fist;
the cross will safeguard the victories thereof;
her cherished children abide at her breast,
where we feed on her milk of faith and love.

Let us strengthen her arms and heart still more,
and keep in motion this cradle of peaks;
we'll forge her arms of iron for times of war,
yet fill her breast with love for times of peace.

Country! victory's wings have lifted you upward;
your orb now rises like a golden sun;
now turn the chariot of your glory westward,
O Catalonia! since God leads you on.

Forward! by hills, by plains and seas press on,
the Pyrenees have grown too small for throne;
today you waken shadowed in the cross
               to come into your own.

EPILOGUE. THE TWO BELL TOWERS

Superb abbeys, what has come of you all?
Marcèvol, Serrabona, Sant Miquel,
And crumbling Sant Martí, who with your strains
Of psalm and melody once filled the vale,
Seeding earth with angels, and sky with saints?

What has become of all your cloisters, O dales,
That served so long the love of Christ for school?
Where, O solitude, is your psalter now?
Where, sanctuary, do your monks now file,
As body without soul you lie in sorrow?

What of the room where Orseolo slept?
And what of great Garí's abbatial cell?
And what of Romualdo's oratory,
And palliums and retables richly set
A thousand years ago in gold and ivory?

Your canticles now silent, your lights extinguished,
The petals of your shining rose are shed,
Your harps and holy hymns all sleeping long,
Like yellowhammers, lifeless in their nest,
Just when the wood rang clear in sparkling song.

Of altars Romanesque lie no remains,
Your cloister, Byzantine, has left no trace,
Bright alabaster fallen long ago,
The lamp that shone is but an orb effaced
That nevermore will grace Mount Canigó.

Just like two giants from some saintly army,
Alone upon the land there rise two belfries:
Last among the monks to make their departure,
They turn their gaze again, before the leaving,
Upon the ruins of what were once their altars.

Two stalwart sentinels is what they are,
Now posted in Conflent, eternal guards:
Tall oak trees seem like bramble at their feet,
And stone-built dwellings rising on the swards
Below these bulking herdsmen seem like sheep.

One pitch-dark night the tower of Cuixà hailed
His brother: "Could it be your voice has failed?
Each hour your song would rouse me with its ringing;
Our voices as they blended through the vale
Would lift our praise and thanks to God each morning."

"I have no more bells," came down the reply
From sturdy Sant Martí high on the rise.
"But were one day my bells restored to me,
They'd toll for all my monks gone off to die:
For all my monks gone off to die, and me.

"How heavy were their hearts the day they left!
All afternoon I watched them as they wept,
And seven times looked back from down the path;
A hundred years this vigil now I've kept:
Might you, below, have seen them coming back?"

"No, the miners only, and plowmen take
The Codalet and Prada roads: they say
That every clutch one day returns to tree,
But those who from our branches went their way
Will lift no more their song of love so sweet.

"No more! for now they lie within the earth,
While we, too, above them, tumble downward;
Abandoned by the century we upraised,
Our fame in its oblivion interred,
Our bones, our glory, our memory betrayed."

"Alas! my chapels it has turned to stables,
And cast to shifting winds the venerable
Ashes of the Count of Rià, my founder;
Devils have dislodged the work of angels,
Who flew to weep in sorrow on the mountain.

"And I wept with them, and I sorrow still,
Alas! all hope of solace lost with all
That was: and gone now all that I desired,
I stand and watch my petals as they fall,
A beeless hive, the stir within has died."

"We'll fall together," Cuixà's tower replies.
"Long stood another belfry by my side;
Lifting his broad head, he rivaled the summits,
Sounding wide his voice: now bold, now mild,
Now a crashing tempest, now shrilling trumpets.

"Like mine, his life had spanned nine hundred years,
Yet like Methuselah's, his death drew near,
And like Goliath struck upright full force,
He fell headlong, and now upon his bier
Calls out to me, a vast unburied corpse.

"And soon my skeleton, deformed and wrecked,
Will lie undone and bleached in Codalet;
My head weighs heavy, and with night advancing,
When rising up to make her vesper visit,
The moon marvels to find me here still standing.

"I too will go and rest, and from your hilltop
You too one day will join me on this spot,
And those whose plows above our graves make good
Will never say, nor guess, what was our lot,
Where Sant Miquel and Sant Martí once stood."

So spoke the pair of belfries there that night;
But next day, at dawn, in the morning sunlight,
Taking up the strains left off in the vale,
The ringdove stopped to converse with the ivy,
The daystar to chat with the nightingale.

Heartened, the mountain smiled down on the scene,
And boasting a burgeoning cloak of green,
Shone like a bride all decked with jewels and gems,
Then doffed a thousand snowdrifts from its mien
Just like an orange sapling snowy blossoms.

What one century builds up, the next brings low,
But God's enduring monument stands long;
Nor raging winds, nor war, nor wrath of men
Will overturn the peaks of Canigó:
The soaring Pyrenees will not be bent.

Annotated index

Abd ar-Rahman, or Abd ar-Rahman Al-Ghafiqi, emir of Córdoba, who having crushed a Berber revolt in Cerdanya led by Abu-Nezah in 731, marched into Gaul, defeated Eudes at Bordeaux, sacked Gascony, Touraine and Poitou, and was finally routed by Charles Martel at the Battle of Tours (732); in *Lampegia*, c.7.

Abu-Nezah, or Munuza, Berber governor who allied himself with Aquitaine, wedded Duke Eudes's daughter, and led a revolt against Abd ar-Rahman in 731; in *Lampegia*, c.7 (see *Abd ar-Rahman*).

Adam, 'Adam's fall' depicted on the portal of Santa Maria de Ripoll: c.11.

Adela, also Adelaida, c.11 (see *Guillem I de Besalú*).

Africa, in the *Passage of Hannibal*, c.7.

Aglí, river emerging in the Corberes flowing SE then E into the Mediterranean N of Perpinyà: in *Rosselló*, c.6; and the faerie of Galamús: c.6; c.12.

Alberes, faerie of, in the *Passage of Hannibal*, c.7.

Alberes, the, mountain range (1263 m / 4143 ft) running E-W at the eastern end of the Pyrenees, separating Rosselló from Alt Empordà; compared with La Maladeta in *La Maladeta*, c.4; in *Rosselló*, c.6 (see *Alberes, faerie of*).

Alhambra, Moorish palace and fortress built on the outskirts of Granada in the twelfth and thirteenth centuries under the Nasrid dynasty; compared with Flordeneu's palace: c.3; compared with the faeries' marble mountain hall: c.6.

Almansor, or al-Mansur, hagib of Córdoba (r.978-1002), assaulted and sacked Barcelona under Borrell II in 985, prompting the Catalan counties to strengthen their ties with the Frankish kingdom; Gentil fought against with his father Tallaferro: c.1; invoked by Oliba: c.12.

Alós, valley in NW Pallars Sobirà (E of La Vall d'Aran) through which the Noguera Pallaresa runs southward; in *Noguera and Garona,* c.7.

Alp, or Tosa d'Alp, mountain (2531 m / 8303 ft) situated in SE Baixa Cerdanya: c.4.

Alps, in the *Passage of Hannibal,* c.7.

Amalekites, depicted on the portal of Santa Maria de Ripoll: c.11.

Amand, Bagaudian king; and the faerie of Ribes: c.6; Verdaguer notes: *'the Bagaudians held up near the caves of Ribes until the Gothic troops under Euric seized Amand, their chieftain or king, and slew him on the summit of Foixera, called the Plateau of Amand, where the ruins of a primitive fortress can still be seen.'*

Amazon, legendary woman warrior; Catalonia compared to by Oliba: c.12.

Andorra, 'Andorran timberlands': invoked by the faerie of Fontargent: c.12.

Aneto, (see *Neto*).

Angel, 'An Angel overhead': guardian spirits were sometimes attributed by Verdaguer to collective identities or geographic features; here, guardian of the homeland and custodian of amity, identified with the Pyrenees: in *La Maladeta,* c.4.

Angostrina, (Fr. *Angoustrine*), village NW of Llívia; in *Lampegia,* c.7.

April, personified: c.1, 3, 4, 9, 11, 12.

Aquae Grani, today the city of Aachen (Germany), seat of Charlemagne's empire; in *Eixalada,* c.9.

Aquitania, or Aquitaine, duchy in SW France; in *Lampegia,* c.7.

Araby, Arabic-speaking lands; in *Lampegia,* c.7.

Aran, c.4 (see *Vall d'Aran*).

Archangel, the, in *Eixalada,* c.9 (see *Saint Michael*).

Argelers, (Fr. *Argèles-sur-Mer*), town in Rosselló near the seabord SE of Elna: c.5.

Argenteria, one of several canyon walls in Collegats whose curious features have given rise to local legend: c.4.

Ariadne, 'Ariadne's splendorous crown': crown of stars (Corona Borealis or Northern Crown) promised to Ariadne by Dionysus, whom she wedded after being abandoned on Naxos by Theseus: invoked by the hermit of Meritxell: c.12.

Ark of the Covenant, depicted on the portal of Santa Maria de Ripoll: c.11.

Arles, (Fr. *Arles-sur-Tech*), town on the Tec SE of the Canigó massif; its Benedictine monastery (founded 778) is Catalonia's oldest Carolingian abbey; in *Rosselló*, c.6.

Armenroda, northern area of the Cap de Creus peninsula; and the faerie of Banyoles: c.6; Coromines suggests a Celtic etymology: *are-moni-rotas*, 'near/east of Mount Roda' (see *Sant Pere de Roda*).

Arrià, or Rià (Fr. *Ria*), town on the River Tet N of Cornellà; today only partial foundations remain of the castle that once stood on the town's western hill: c.2; sacked by Saracens: c.7 (see *Rià*).

Arse, valley and waterfall (1485–1390 m / 4872–4560 ft) in Ariège (France): c.4.

Aspres, mountain range branching NNE from the E side of the Canigó massif: c.8 (see *Cameles*).

Asturias, first independent Christian kingdom in Muslim Spain under Pelayo (see *Pelayo*), marking the beginning of the Christian conquest of the Iberian peninsula; in *La Maladeta*, c.4.

Atlantic (Ocean), in *Noguera and Garona*, c.7.

Atlas (mountains), Hannibal compared with 'Atlas mountain lions' in the *Passage of Hannibal*, c.7.

Aubé, mountain lake (2085 m / 6840 ft) above the valley of Arse in Ariège (France): c.4.

Ausona, Latin name for modern county of Osona (see *Vic*); invoked by St. Lucian and St. Marcian: c.12.

Bagaudian, c.6 (see *Amand*).

Balaguer, city on the River Segre NE of Lleida; in *Noguera and Garona*, c.7.

Balaig, fir-timbered valley on the N slope of Canigó drained by the Llitera: c.8.

Balearians, in Hannibal's army, warriors from the Balearic Islands renowned for their skill in using slings: in the *Passage of Hannibal,* c.7.

Banyoles, faerie of, tells of Lake Banyoles and presents Gentil with a wedding veil: c.6; c.12.

Banyoles, Lake, (Cat. *Estany de Banyoles*), situated on the plain below the Rocacorba mountain range NW of Girona; home of the fairie of Banyoles: c.6.

Banyoles, monastery of, dedicated to St. Stephen (Cat. *Sant Esteve de Banyoles*), dating from at least the eighth century; monks of Banyoles speak: c.12.

Banyuls, (Fr. *Banyuls-sur-Mer*), seabord town in SE Rosselló; in the *Passage of Hannibal,* c.7; c.8.

Barcelona, construction of the present-day cathedral began in 1298, but the façade and crossing tower were not undertaken until 1885, the year of *Canigó*'s publication, and completed in 1913: in *La Maladeta,* c.4; and the faerie of Mirmanda: c.6; and Count Pelós: c.11 (see *Guifré el Pelós*); invoked by Saint Eulària: c.12 (see *Saint Eulària*); and Count Berenguer: c.12 (see *Berenguer Ramon I of Barcelona*).

Barrès, Tet river valley in Alta Cerdanya (France) stretching southeasterly from Lake Bollosa (Fr. *Lac des Bouillouses*) SE of the Carlit massif; in *Eixalada,* c.9.

Basins, (Cat. Bacins), Verdaguer notes: *'the "faeries' basins" are pools inside the cave of Sirac'* (see *Sirac*): c.6.

Bastera, cave above the confluence of the Tet and Cadí rivers at Vilafranca (Fr. *Villefranche-de-Conflent*) NW of the Canigó massif: c.6 (see *Sirac*).

Bay of Biscay, in *A Saint John's Bouquet,* c.1.

Bedouin, 'Bedouin dreams' in description of the Canigó massif: c.2.

Beget, village in NE Ripollès E of Camprodon, renowned for its twelfth-century wood sculpture of the Crucifixion: c.5.

Begur, mountains of, coastal range E of Girona in Baix Empordà below the Ter estuary: c.6; invoked by the faeries of Roses and Banyoles: c.12.

Begur, town near the Mediterranean coast E of Girona; and the faerie of Banyoles: c.6.

Bellcaire, (Oc. *Bèucaire,* Fr. *Beaucaire*) town in Languedoc-Roussillon (France) on the Rhone; Tallaferro's journey: c.11.

Benasc, or Benasca, Pyrenean valley circling N of La Maladeta in Osca (Sp. *Huesca*): c.4.

Benedictines, the Benedictine rule was imposed throughout the Carolingian Empire in 817; c.6.

Berenguer Ramon I of Barcelona, (c.1006-1035), count of Barcelona; invoked by Oliba: c.12.

Beret, mountain valley (1860 m / 6100 ft) in NW Pallars Sobirà where the Noguera Pallarès and Garona rivers emerge; in *Noguera and Garona,* c.7.

Besalú, seat of the historic county of Besalú in NE Catalonia and central Rosselló established in 894 by Guifré el Pelós; c.8, 9.

Besiberri, mountain massif (3030 m / 9940 ft) in northern Alta Ribagorça bordering La Vall d'Aran, separating the valleys of Boí and Barravés: c.4.

Betera, or Batera (also Vetera), defense tower in the eastern Canigó massif on a hill rising 1523 m / 4996 ft E of Estella Peak; c.2, 9.

Blessed Virgin's Church, the crypt dedicated to the Blessed Virgin (consecrated in 1009) lies beneath the main church of Sant Martí del Canigó (consecrated in 1026): c.11.

Boera, canal running NE from Serdinyà near the Tet: c.6.

Boí, mountain valley in the county of Alta Ribagorça, NW Catalonia: c.4.

Boniface IV, Pope, (c.550-615), invoked by the monks of Sant Pere de Roda: c.12 (see *Sant Pere de Roda*).

Book of Seven Seals, (from Rev. 5:1; 5:5; 6:1); depicted on the portal of Santa Maria de Ripoll: c.11.

Bordeaux, in *Noguera and Garona,* c.7.

Bresca, hamlet in Collegats S of Gerri on the Noguera Pallaresa: c.4.

Bugarac, mountain peak (1230 m / 4035 ft) in the Corberes range near the source of the Aglí NW of Sant Pau de Fenollet; the faerie of Galamus's necklace of topaz from Bugarac: c.6.

Bullosa, today a reservoir formed by a dam built in 1902; formerly, vast marshlands stretching eastward from Carlit and flowing into the Tet: c.4.

Cabdella, mountain valley in northern Pallars Jussà W of Montsent Peak: c.4.

Cabo Higuer, promontory in the Bay of Biscay N of the town of Hondarribia at the W end of the Pyrenees: c.4.

Cabrenç, or Cabrenys, fortress that stood SW of Serrallonga (Fr. *Serralongue*), Vallespir's major castle during the early medieval period, cited in 1086 as *castrum Serralonga*: c.2; Tallaferro calls to arms: c.5.

Cabrera, Castle of, today little remains of the former castle (first cited eleventh century) that stood atop a cliff (849 m / 2785 ft) overlooking the broad plain of Empordà NE of Maçanet de Cabrenys: c.5.

Cadí,[1] pre-Pyrenean mountain range (2608 m / 8556 ft) stretching 40km E-W, SE of La Seu d'Urgell in the counties of Baixa Cerdanya, Berguedà and Alt Urgell: c.4.

Cadí,[2] (Fr. *Cady*), affluent of the Tec emerging in the Vale of Cadí: c.9; Guifre's cell looks out on: c.11.

Cadí, Vale of, (Cat. *Vall de Cadí*), mountain valley formed by a glacial cirque on the western side of the Canigó massif and drained by the Cadí; home to Canigó's faeries: c.2; Gentil falls to his death: c.7.

Cadinell, southern spur (2112 m / 6929 ft) of the Cadí range in Alt Urgell: c.4; Verdaguer notes: *'not so rocky, lusher, and lower than Cadí, of which it seems a tender shoot.'*

Cameles, (Fr. *Camélas*), ridge rising above the Tet river valley at the northern end of the Aspres: c.8; Verdaguer notes: *'[its] shape is somewhat like that of a camel, and on its enormous hump stands a hermitage devoted to Saint Martin lording it over the countryside.'*

Camp, monastery of Santa Maria del, founded 1090, NE of the village of Paçà (Fr. *Passa*) in Rosselló, whose monks speak in c.12 (see *Field*).

Camprodon, town in NE Ripollès where the Ter and Ritort rivers meet; its Benedictine monastery was founded c.950 by Guifré I of Besalú, Tallaferro's great-grandfather: c.4.

Campsaure, mountain peak (2142 m / 7027 ft) in La Vall d'Aran along the W border with Haute-Garonne (France): c.4.

Canigó, (*ca-nee-GO*), (Fr. *Canigou*), highest peak (2784 m / 9137 ft) in the Canigó massif at the eastern end of the Pyrenees; c.1; Gentil's ascent: c.2; c.3; in *La Maladeta*, c.4; c.5; in *Rosselló*, c.6; in *Song of Gentil*, c.7; Guifre finds Gentil: c.7; Guifre reassembles the dispersed militia: c.8; c.9, 10; construction of the monastery of Sant Martí del Canigó: c.11; abandoned by the faeries and claimed by Oliba and his followers who plant the Cross of Canigó at the summit: c.12; abandoned abbeys and priories of, in closing lines: epilogue.

Canigó in blossom, (Cat. *'Muntanyes regalades'*), poem in c.6; Verdaguer makes use of a popular *ranz*: *'Muntanyes regalades / són les del Canigó, / que tot l'estiu floreixen, / primavera i tardor. / Dau-me l'amor, minyona, / dau-me lo vostre cor!* (…).

Cannae, battle of, Hannibal's victory over the Romans in the Second Punic War (216 BC): in the *Passage of Hannibal,* c.7.

Cap de Creus, Catalonia's easternmost promontory where the Pyrenean foothills descend to the Mediterranean NE of Roses: in *La Maladeta,* c.4.

Capcir, county W of Conflent: c.1; Guifre reassembles militia: c.8; in *Eixalada,* c.9.

Capitoline, city of the, Rome, invoked by the monks of Sant Pere de Roda: c.12.

Carançà, or Carrançà, mountain pass (2727 m / 8947 ft) on the Northern Catalonian border E of Giant Pit's Peak, separating the Carançà cirque and river valley (Conflent) and the Coma de Vaca valley (Ripollès): c.8.

Carlit, massif and highest peak (2921 m / 9583 ft) in the eastern Pyrenees in Alta Cerdanya (France); Gentil's ascent with Flordeneu, c.4; compared with La Maladeta in *La Maladeta,* c.4.

Carthage, in the *Passage of Hannibal,* c.7.

Castell, or Castell de Vernet (Fr. *Casteil*), village in the county of Conflent W of the Canigó massif: c.1; sacked by Saracens: c.7.

Castelló, Castelló d'Empúries, town in Alt Empordà county W of Roses renowned for its early medieval bishopric and dynastic line of counts; c.5 (see *Ogier*).

Castile, c.4.

Catalan(s), 'Catalan homeland': c.4; 'Catalans' in *La Maladeta,* c.4; 'Catalan Stripes': c.10; 'Catalan mountains': c.12.

Catalan Stripes, c.10 (see *Four Stripes*).

Catalonia, Abd ar-Rahman sets out for: in *Lampegia,* c.7; 'Catalonia's heart,' 'Catalonia's arch': c.11; invoked by chorus of monks, Oliba, faeries, St. Damasus, and final chorus: c.12.

Caucoliberis, in *Rosselló,* c.6 (see *Cotlliure*).

Celtiberians, Celtic-speaking inhabitants of (pre-Roman) Iberia: in *La Maladeta*, c.4.

Cerdanya, historic county in Northern Catalonia held by Muslims until the Carolingian Empire established a foothold in the ninth century. The modern county of Alta (*upper*) Cerdanya lies W of Conflent, today part of Northern Catalonia (France); extending southward, Baixa (*lower*) Cerdanya is today a county in Catalonia; Guifre II Count of Cerdanya: c.1; various descriptions: c.4; in *Rosselló*, c.6; in the *Passage of Hannibal* and *Lampegia*, c.7; Guifre reassembles militia: c.8; in *Eixalada*, c.9; Guisla, Countess of Cerdanya: c.10; faeries bid farewell and Christendom takes hold, invoked by St. Damasus: c.12.

Ceret, (Fr. *Céret*), town in Vallespir on the Tec E of the Canigó massif: c.5; its Romanesque bridge (1321), known as the Pont del Diable (*Devil's Bridge*), has a single arch 45 m (nearly 150 ft) in length: c.8.

Charlemagne, (742-814), in Oliba's legendary account, sponsors the founding of Sant Miquel de Cuixà following the destruction of Eixalada: in *Eixalada*, c.9; invoked by the monks of the monastery of Camp, invoked by the monks of Banyoles: c.12.

Chosroes, or Chosroes II, king of Persia (r.590-628), whose armies seized Jerusalem, as told by the monks of Sant Pere de Roda: c.12.

Christian(s), c.5, 6; in *Lampegia*, c.7; c.8, 9.

Clota Florida, (Fr. *Clote Fouride*), mountain peak (2373 m / 7785 ft) NE of Andorra; and the faerie of Fontargent: c.6.

Coç, fortress now in ruins atop Montalé Hill NE of the village of El Tec, cited in 1340 as *la forsa de Munt Alé*. c.2.

Codalet, village in Conflent (France) by Sant Miquel de Cuixà; c.9; epilogue.

Coll d'Ares, mountain pass (1513 m / 4964 ft) along the Northern Catalonian border NW of Camprodon: c.8.

Collegats, narrow canyon carved by the Noguera Pallaresa in S Pallars Sobirà: c.4.

Collet Verd, mountain pass on the W side of the Canigó massif: c.5.

Coma d'Or, mountain peak (2826 m / 9271 ft) in Alta Cerdanya: c.4.

Coma Ermada, peak (1996 m / 6548 ft) in the Montgrony range; and the faerie of Ribes: c.6.

Comalada, valley and stream dropping SE from Tretzevents into the Tec; c.2, 5, 9.

Conflenç, or Coflens, (Occitan, *Couflens*), village in Ariège (France) E of Mt Vallier: c.4.

Conflent, county in the E Pyrenees W of Rosselló (France), heart of the historic county of Cerdanya: c.1, 10, 11, epilogue.

Corberes, (Fr. *Corbières*), mountain range N of Rosselló joining the Pyrenees near the River Aude; in *Rosselló*, c.6; and the faerie of Galamús: c.6.

Cornellà, or Cornellà de Conflent, (Fr. *Corneilla-de-Conflent*), village S of the River Tet in the Cornellà valley NW of Canigó; residence of Guifre: c.2, 6; sacked by Saracens: c.7; Guifre bids farewell to Guisla: c.10.

Costabona, Pyrenean massif and peak (2465 m / 8087 ft) on the Northern Catalonian border separating the Tec and Ter river valleys: c.4.

Costoges, or Costoja, (Fr. *Coustouges*), village in S Vallespir E of the Castle of Cabrenç: c.5.

Cotlliure, (Fr. *Collioure*), seabord town in SE Rosselló, cited in the seventh century as *castrum Caucoliberi* – from the Ibero-Basque *Caucoliberis*, suggesting that Cotlliure was the port for *Illiberis* (see *Elna*) – and fortified under the Carolingians; Tallaferro's capture and escape: c.5; in *Rosselló*, c.6; Guifre sights burning galleys: c.8; invoked by St. Vincent: c.12.

Count Arnau, (Cat. *el Comte Arnau*), legendary figure, widely celebrated in lore, literature and musical works, whose origins lie in a popular ballad from the Ripoll area: invoked by the faerie of Ribes: c.12.

Count of Cerdanya, c.1 (see *Guifre II of Cerdanya*).

Count's Spring, the (Cat. *la Font del Comte*), below Sant Martí del Canigó, a sculpted bronze plaque now depicts Verdaguer with his contemporary Juli de Carsalade, bishop of Perpinyà; c.1, 9.

Crabera, mountain range and peak (2557 m / 8389 ft) NNW of Beret separating La Vall d'Aran and Ariège (France); in *Noguera and Garona*, c.7.

Crate, the, (Cat. *la Caixa*), dolmen situated below the Pebbles, on the N slopes of the Tec river valley NW of Arles: c.8.

Cross of Canigó, Guifre asks Oliba to plant on Canigó's summit: c.11; planted on the summit: c.12.

Crux fidelis, inter omnes / Arbor una nobilis, (Faithful cross, of all trees most noble), from the sixth-century hymn attributed to Venantius Fortunatus; spoken by chorus of saints among the clouds: c.12.

Cuixà, (see *Sant Miquel de Cuixà*), in *Eixalada*, c.9; invoked by Abbot Garí: c.12; personified: epilogue.

Damascus, in *Lampegia*, c.7.

Daniel, invoked by chorus of monks: c.12.

David, depicted on the portal of Santa Maria de Ripoll: c.11.

David, city of, Jerusalem, seized by Chosroes II in 614; invoked by the monks of Sant Pere de Roda: c.12.

December, 'Like sunrays in December mist' in description of Flordeneu's hair: c.2.

Delilah, compared with Flordeneu: c.7.

Dhaulagiri, Himalayan massif, once thought to be the world's highest mountain: compared with La Maladeta in *La Maladeta*, c.4.

Diana, compared with Lampegia in *Lampegia*, c.7.

Dies Irae, or Day of Wrath, medieval poem depicting Judgment Day; in Guifre's dreams: c.11.

Doris, daughter of Oceanus and Tethys; in *Rosselló*, c.6 (see *Nereids*).

Dryads, wood nymphs; in *Rosselló*, c.6.

Ebre, (Sp. *Ebro*), major river emerging in the Cantabrian Mountains, flowing southeasterly gathering waters from the Pyrenees and emptying into the Mediterranean at the Delta de l'Ebre, SE of Tortosa; in *La Maladeta*, c.4.

Eina, c.4 (see *Vale of Eina*).

Eixalada, ancient Benedictine monastery Sant Andreu d'Eixalada in northern Conflent along the Tet (cited 840) destroyed by flooding in 878, and whose surviving monks founded Sant Miquel de Cuixà; c.9.

Eixalada, poem in c.9 narrated mostly by Oliba giving the legendary account of the destruction of the monastery of Eixalada and founding of the monastery at Cuixà.

El Cid, Rodrigo Díaz de Vivar, '*El Cid Campeador,*' eleventh-century hero celebrated in the Spanish epic *Cantar de Mio Cid*; in *La Maladeta*, c.4.

El Portús, (today, El Pertús), (Fr. *Le Perthus*), mountain pass and town along the Northern Catalonian border at the W end of the Alberes range: c.8.

Elena, c.1 (see *Elna*).

Elija, depicted on the portal of Santa Maria de Ripoll: c.11.

Elna, (Fr. *Elne*), town north of the River Tec near the seabord, bishopric from the sixth century until the nineteenth century when it was superseded by Perpinyà; cited by Livy as *Illiberis*, from the Ibero-Basque *Iri-berri or* 'new town'; Verdaguer notes: *'the city of Elena, or Elna, was named* Castrum Helenæ *by Constantine in memory of his mother*,' attacked by Saracens: c.1; built upon the ivory palace of Tethys: in *Rosselló*, c.6.

Els Encantats, massif and twin peaks (2747 m, 2738 m / 9012 ft, 8982 ft) in Pallars Sobirà, separating La Noguera Pallaresa and La Noguera de Tor (Alta Ribagorça) river basins: c.4; Verdaguer notes: *'according to tradition, the peaks are hunters turned to stone as punishment for missing Mass one Sunday while out chasing an izard.'*

Els Horts, former hamlet in the Tet river valley NW of Canigó, whose name means *gardens*, irrigated by a spring; the remains of its fifteenth-century castle lie atop Puig Mitjà; in the *Passage of Hannibal,* c.7.

Empordà, two counties in NE Catalonia, Alt Empordà and Baix Empordà; crowned by Begur, Armenroda, Puig Neulós, Mont and Rocacorba: c.5; and the faerie of Banyoles, and the faerie of Roses: c.6; invoked by St. Damasus: c.12.

Empúries, ancient city on the Mediterranean seabord NE of Girona, founded c.600 BC by Phocaeans from Asia Minor or Massalia (Marseilles) superseded by the Roman settlement *Emporiae* in the late third century BC: c.4.

Enveig the Knight, d', (Cat. *el cavaller d'Enveig*), legendary knight from Enveig, village in Alta Cerdanya (France) NNW of Puigcerdà, whose encounter with the faerie of Lanós led to the destruction of Eixalada: in *Eixalada*, c.9.

Erin, Ireland; in *Eixalada*, c.9.

Espot, or Portarró d'Espot, narrow mountain pass (Cat. *Portarró d'Espot*) NW of Els Encantats: c.4.

Esquerda, mountain range E of Sant Pau de Fenollet separating the Aglí from the Maurí river valley to the north: c.6.

Éssera, river emerging in La Maladeta massif, flowing southwesterly through Benasc and joining the Cinca and the Segre further south; in *La Maladeta*, c.4.

Esterri, plain of, in *Noguera and Garona*, c.7 (see *Roland's mace*).

Estunes, situated W of Lake Banyoles; and the faerie of Banyoles: c.6; Verdaguer notes: *'the Estunes are a great ridge of rock broken up long ago by an earthquake, and in whose huge cracks, they say, stood faeries' palaces.'*

Ethiopians, in the *Passage of Hannibal*, c.7.

Eudes, duke of Aquitaine who allied himself with Abu-Nezah to whom he gave his daughter in wedlock, later swearing allegiance to Charles Martel after the Battle of Poitiers (731); in *Lampegia*, c.7 (see *Abd ar-Rahman, Abu-Nezah, Lampegia*).

Europe, in the *Passage of Hannibal*, c.7.

Evangelists, four, Matthew, Mark, Luke, John; c.11.

Fallen Angel, the, in *La Maladeta*, c.4.

Fenolledes, or La Fenolleda, county in Northern Catalonia (France), invoked by the faerie of Galamús: c.12 (see *Sant Pau de Fenolleda*).

Field, the, (Cat. *El Camp*), Verdaguer notes that *Galamús* comes from the Latin *campus*, meaning 'field': c.6.

Finestrelles Pass, (Cat. *Coll de Finestrelles*), mountain pass (2604 m / 8543 ft) in the Puigmal massif along the chain of peaks separating Alta and Baixa Cerdanya: c.4.

firespinners, (Cat. *fallaires*): c.1, 5: Verdaguer notes: *'in some Pyrenean valleys on the eve of Saint John's, firespinners run in file through woods and mountainsides brandishing torches or firebrands, chanting and singing in honor of Saint John ...'*

Flecte ramos, arbor alta, (Bend down your branches, lofty tree), from the sixth-century hymn attributed to Venantius Fortunatus; spoken by chorus of saints among the clouds: c.12.

Flordeneu, (*flow-duh-NAY-oo*), (literally 'snowflower'), meaning 'snow-drop' (*Galanthus nivalis*), queen of Canigó's faeries who takes on the appearance of Griselda to deceive Gentil and hold him prisoner in love: c.2; rides with Gentil in her flying chariot above the Pyrenees: c.4; shows Gentil Rosselló from the summit of Canigó: c.6; prepares to wed Gentil, discovers his lifeless body, mourns his death and vows revenge: c.7; c.9; driven from Canigó by Oliba: c.12.

Font de la Regina, or Font dels Enamorats, legendary site of Abu-Nezah's death; in *Lampegia*, c.7.

Font-romeu, sanctuary dedicated to Our Lady of Font-romeu, whose wooden image dates from the thirteenth century, located in the village of Font-romeu in Alta Cerdanya (France); invoked by the provosts of Núria and Font-romeu: c.12.

Font Viva, or Fontviva, stream flowing westward off the Carlit massif: c.4.

Fontalba, mountain pass SE of Puigmal; invoked with its rivers by the faerie of Fontargent: c.12.

Fontargent, mountain peak (2619 m / 8592 ft) in NE Andorra along the border with Ariège (France): c.4; and the faerie of Fontargent: c.6; invoked with its nearby lakes by the faerie of Fontargent: c.12.

Fontargent, faerie of, tells of meeting a panner and presents Gentil with a wedding ring: c.6; tells the tale *Noguera and Garona*, c.7; speaks: c.12.

Forana, Gate of, (Cat. *Porta Forana*), 'outer gate' leading to the path skirting the western base of the Canigó massif: c.5.

Força-real, sanctuary of *La Mare de Déu de la Força-real,* built on the remains of the former tower of Montner between the Aglí and Tet river valleys; in *Rosselló*, c.6.

Fount Cristall, (Cat. *Font de Cristall*), spring located in an ice cave near La Canal del Cristall Peak (2586 m / 8484 ft) in the Cadí range: c.4.

Four Stripes, the legendary origins of the present-day Catalan flag, four red stripes on a yellow field, date from the ninth century: c.1 (see *Guifré el Pelós*; 'Catalan Stripes': c.10).

France, in *La Maladeta*, c.4; in *Noguera and Garona*, c.7; invoked by chorus of monks: c.12.

Freser, river flowing southward gathering waters from the valleys of Núria and Ribes then joining the Ter S of Ripoll: c.4; and the faerie of Ribes: c.6; c.12.

Fullà, town and nearby caves in the Tet river valley NW of Canigó: c.6.

Galamús, spectacular ravines with caves carved by the Aglí along a fault at Sant Pau de Fenollet: c.6 (see *Field*).

Galamús, faerie of, tells of Galamús and presents Gentil with a topaz necklace: c.6; speaks: c.12.

Garí, also Garin, renowned tenth-century abbot of Cuixà who brought Orseolo to the abbey (see *Orseolo*); in *Eixalada,* c.9; speaks: c.12; epilogue.

Garona, (Fr. *Garonne*), river emerging in E La Vall d'Aran, passing west-ward through Viella before flowing northward into France and into the Atlantic NW of Bordeaux; in *La Maladeta,* c.4; in *Noguera and Garona,* c.7 (see *Noguera and Garona*).

Gedhur, or the Giant, Saracen captain defeated by Guifre: c.8 (see *Giant's Pit*).

Gentil, (*jen-TEEL*), son of Tallaferro; Verdaguer's invention inspired loosely in the legendary Cavaller d'Enveig, whose encounter with a fay led to the disaster at the Benedictine monastery of Eixalada, destroyed by floods in 878 (see *Eixalada*); knighted by Guifre: c.1; ascends Mount Canigó and held captive by Flordeneu: c.2-3; ride with Flordeneu in her flying chariot above the Pyrenees: c.4; Tallaferro invokes: c.5; c.6; falls to his death: c.7 (see *Song of Gentil*); burial: c.9; Griselda and Guisla speak of: c.10; remembered by Guifre, sought by Griselda: c.11; his spirit descends to meet Guifre's: c.12.

Gerri, cascades: c.4.

Gerri, (**Santa Maria de**), twelfth-century monastery on the Noguera Pallaresa near the town of Gerri de la Sal; in *Noguera and Garona,* c.7.

Giant's Pit, the, (Cat. *La Fossa del Gegant*), Pyrenean depression (2605 m / 8546 ft) in Conflent NNW of Giant's Pit Peak; legendary tomb of Gedhur: c.8; Verdaguer notes: *'The Giant's Pit was a dolmen situated at the bottom of the depression by the same name, made of four rocks forming a small square. The further rock was about one and a half meters long, while the sides were a bit longer and leaned inward to serve as both walls and roof. At the front stood a smaller rock… more regular in shape and of a different type, suggesting it was added later by someone seeking shelter in modern times… One day some shepherds saw their humble shelter being examined by some gentlemen from Barcelona who took great care in measuring and drawing it. Thinking a hidden treasure lay beneath the rocks, they eagerly smashed them to bits, utterly destroying the priceless monument that had given its name to the valley and Giant's peak above.'*

Giant's Pit Peak, (Cat. *Pic de la Fossa del Gegant*), mountain peak (2801 m / 9189 ft) along the Northern Catalonian border NE of the valley of Núria (see *Giant's Pit*).

Girona, major city in NE Catalonia and bishopric since the early sixth century; according to tradition, the city was liberated in 785 by Charlemagne, who established the historic county as a defense zone known as the Spanish March: c.4; invoked by monks of Banyoles, by St. Narcissus: c.12.

Goa, or Goà, signal tower standing W of Castell, cited in 1389 as *turris de Goa*: c.2.

Golgotha, Calvary; 'Golgotha's blossoming tree,' the Cross; invoked by chorus of monks: c.12.

Goliath, in *La Maladeta*, c.4; compared with Gedhur: c.9; compared to the fallen bell tower of Cuixà by Cuixà's remaining tower: epilogue.

Griselda, shepherdess; Verdaguer's invention; her love for Gentil angers Tallaferro: c.1; Flordeneu takes on her appearance to deceive Gentil: c.2; in *Song of Gentil*, c.7; learns of Gentil's death: c.10; roams the mountainsides in search of Gentil: c.11.

Guifré el Pelós, nickname for Guifré I (c.840-897), (aka Wilfred the Hairy), Count of Cerdanya, Urgell, Barcelona, Girona and Besalú; following the devastating incursions (827) of Abu Marwan, Guifré consolidated the Catalan counties, fostering Christian repopulation southward from the Pyrenees and founding the monasteries at Ripoll and Sant Joan de les Abadesses; threatened by Ismail ibn Musa after nearly thirty years of peace, Guifré mounted an offensive and suffered fatal wounds while intercepting a foray led by the governor of Lleida; according to legend, Louis the Pious of France placed his hand on the wounded count and traced his four fingers daubed with blood along Guifré's shield, forming the four stripes of the Catalan flag; c.2; and the portal of Santa Maria de Ripoll: c.11.

Guifre II of Cerdanya, (*GEE-fruh*), (also Guifré, c.970-1050), brother of Tallaferro and Oliba, and uncle to Gentil, whom he knights: c.1; finds Gentil on Canigó and sends him to his death: c.7; pursues Saracens and defeats Gedhur: c.8; forgiven by Tallaferro, resolves to found Sant Martí del Canigó and end his days in reclusion: c.9; bids farewell to Guisla: c.10; carves out his tomb and takes ill: c.11; his spirit rises to meet Tallaferro's and Gentil's: c.12.

Guillem I de Besalú, (?-1052), son of Bernat I 'Tallaferro,' weds Adela: c.11.

Guisla, wife of Guifre II: c.7; Guifre bids farewell to, meets Griselda: c.10.

Hagar, (Gen.16:1-16; 21:8-21), Abraham's concubine and mother of Ishmael who in some traditions is Mohammad's ancestor: c.5.

Hannibal, (see *Passage of Hannibal*).

Hole of Sant Ou, (Cat. *Forat de Sant Ou*), crevasse some 80m (260ft) deep near Sant Pere de Montgrony (see *Montgrony*) first explored in 1901; and the faerie of Ribes: c.6.

Hollow of Moixeró, (Cat. *Clot de Moixeró*), Verdaguer notes: '*hidden among the branches of the great Cadí range...[and] carpeted with green grass and blooming jonquil, not a patch of rock shows through and everywhere the hollow babbles with life-giving springs*': c.4.

Iberia, originally, Greek name for Bronze Age peoples of the S and E Iberian peninsula and modern synonym for Spain or the Iberian peninsula: in *La Maladeta,* c.4; Rosselló as gate of: in *Rosselló,* c.6.

Illa, (Fr. *Ille-sur-Têt*), town in the Tet river valley rich in fruit groves: c.3.

Illiberis, in *Rosselló,* c.6 (see *Elna*).

Incles, river valley in NE Andorra: c.4.

Isil, or Gil, village in Pallars Sobirà on the Noguera Pallaresa and site of ninth-century monastery, probably Benedictine: c.4.

Isòvol, village in Baixa Cerdanya famed for its nearby quarries where formerly gray and red marble was extracted: c.3.

Israelites, depicted on the portal of Santa Maria de Ripoll: c.11.

Jehova, in *La Maladeta,* c.4.

Jericho, 'Jericho's walls' depicted on the portal of Santa Maria de Ripoll: c.11.

Jesus, c.9, 11; invoked by St. Damasus: c.12.

Job, invoked by chorus of monks: c.12.

Jonah, depicted on the portal of Santa Maria de Ripoll: c.11.

jongleur, (Cat. *joglar*): c.1; Verdaguer notes: '*in Rosselló, the name "joglars,"*

[L.] "joculatores," *is still given to musicians who play the flabiol, timbrel or bagpipes at local festivals.'*

Joyous, Charlemagne's sword: c.12.

Judas, c.9.

Júlia Llívia, (see *Llívia*).

La Fo,[1] a narrow section of the Galamús ravine at Sant Pau de Fenollet: c.6.

La Fo,[2] (Fr. *Les Gorges de la Fou*), ravine 1700 m (5577 ft) long and 250 m (820 ft) deep near the left bank of the Tec above Arles, today a popular tourist site: c.8.

La Forcada, (today, *La Forcanada or Malh des Pois*), mountain peak (2881 m / 9452 ft) in La Vall d'Aran E of Aneto; compared with La Maladeta: c.4.

La Jonquera, town in N Alt Empordà near the border with Rosselló: c.5.

La Llacuna, today, La Llaguna (Fr. *La Llagonne*), village in Capcir (France) near the southeastern end of the Barrès basin; in *Eixalada,* c.9.

La Regina, sloping grasslands in W Andorra between the Pal and Arinsal rivers: c.4.

La Roca, woods NW of El Portús: c.8.

La Salanca, coastal marshlands N of Perpinyà: c.8.

La Seu d'Urgell, capital of Alt Urgell and the medieval county of Urgell, and bishopric (*seu*) dating from the early sixth century: c.4.

La Tor de Cerdanya, also La Tor de Querol, village in Alta Cerdanya (France) NW of Puigcerdà; in *Eixalada,* c.9.

La Vall d'Aran, (see *Vall d'Aran*).

La Vall d'Arse, c.4 (see *Arse*).

Lampegia, daughter of Duke Eudes of Aquitaine; weds Abu-Nezah, pursued and captured by Abd ar-Rahman: in *Lampegia,* c.7.

Lampegia, tale told by the faerie of Lanós: c.7.

Languedoc, region in southern France; in *Lampegia,* c.7.

Lanós, lake W of Carlit, inhabited by the faerie of Lanós: c.6; in *Eixalada,* c.9.

Lanós, faerie of, presents Gentil with an enchanted golden harp: c.6; tells the tale *Lampegia,* c.7; speaks: c.12.

Laocoöns, 'The damned, these new Laocoöns' depicted on the portal of Santa Maria de Ripoll: c.11.

Les Esqueres, waterfall along the Cadí: c.11.

Lis, valley NNW of La Maladeta in Haute-Garonne (France): c.4.

Lleida, major city in W Catalonia under Muslim rule until 1149: c.8.

Llitera, stream draining northward off the Canigó massif through Balaig into the Tet: c.2.

Llívia, or Júlia Llívia, town belonging to Baixa Cerdanya (Spain) located entirely in Alta Cerdanya (France), known in the first century as *Iulia Lybica*; the old castle (*castrum Libyae quod est Cerritaniae caput*) served as Abu-Nezah's stronghold; in *Lampegia,* c.7 (see *Abu-Nezah*); in *Eïxalada,* c.9.

Llo, formerly fortified village (*castrum de Alloni,* 1095) E of Llívia near the headwaters of the Segre; in *Lampegia,* c.7.

Lot, Abraham's nephew who, aided by angels, fled Sodom with his wife and two daughters (Gen. 19:14-30); invoked by the chorus of monks: c.12.

Lucifer, 'Lucifer's fall' depicted on the portal of Santa Maria de Ripoll: c.11.

Maçana, former watchtower between Argelers (Fr. *Argèles-sur-mer*) and Sureda (Fr. *Sorède*), cited in 1293 as the Tower of Perabona (after St. Peter's Church, cited 981): c.2; in the *Passage of Hannibal,* c.7.

Maçanet, or Maçanet de Cabrenys, mountain village in NW Alt Empordà SSE of the former site of the Castle of Cabrera (see *Roland's mace*): c.5.

Madaloc, hill and signal tower standing SW of Portvendres, cited in 981 as *pogium Madalanco* and reconstructed by the Crown of Aragon, cited in 1340 as *torra de Madaloch*: c.2; Saracens mount surprise attack against Tallaferro: c.5.

Mahomet, c.7, 8; invoked by St. Damasus, by Oliba: c.12.

Mahomet's Bridge, (Cat. *El Pont de Mahoma*), narrow hair-raising ridge climbers straddle to reach the summit of Aneto from the north: in *La Maladeta,* c.4.

Maladeta, la, highest and most rugged massif in the Pyrenees in Osca (Sp. *Huesca*), its several peaks rising above 3000 m / 9842 ft, culminating in Aneto (see *Neto*).

Maladeta, La, poem in c.4.

Marcèvol, twelfth-century priory of Santa Maria de Marcèvol near Arboçols (Fr. *Arboussols*); epilogue.

Marinus, hermit who with Romuald advised Orseolo to leave Venice and live in penitence at Cuixà, where Marinus and Romuald raised a hermitage near the abbey; in *Eixalada,* c.9; speaks: c.12.

Mars, god of war, in the *Passage of Hannibal,* c.7.

Maüt, or La Maüt, (also Sant Martí de Fonollar), pre-Romanesque church (cited 844) featuring twelfth-century murals situated in Morellàs (Fr. *Maureillas-las-Illas*) in the Tec river valley below Ceret; named after Maüt or Mafalda, daughter of Count Ramon Berenguer III of Barcelona (1082-1131), who wedded the viscount of Vallespir: c.8.

May, c.6; personified: c.9, 11; c.12.

Mediterranean (Sea), c.4; in *Noguera and Garona,* c.7.

Meranges, or Portella de Meranges, mountain pass (2647 m / 8684 ft) between Engorgs Peak (2815 m / 9235 ft) and Puigpedrós Peak (2911 m / 9550 ft) connecting Alta and Baixa Cerdanya: c.4; in Rosselló, c.6.

Merialles, plateau on the W side of the Canigó massif where the Cadí and Llipodera valleys meet: c.5.

Meritxell, Our Lady of Meritxell, (Cat. *La Mare de Déu de Meritxell*), patroness of Andorra whose wooden image dates from the twelfth century and whose sanctuary has been rebuilt in the village of Meritxell, central Andorra; invoked by the hermit of Meritxell, speaks: c.12.

Methuselah, compared to Cuixà's fallen bell tower (one of its two original bell towers fell as a result of severe lightning storms in the 1830s): epilogue.

Mirmanda, imaginary ancient city situated in Rosselló near the village of Terrats: c.6; in the *Passage of Hannibal,* c.7; evoked by the faerie of Mirmanda: c.12.

Mirmanda, faerie of, tells of the founding of Mirmanda and presents Gentil with an enchanted mirror: c.6; tells of Hannibal crossing the Pyrenees in the *Passage of Hannibal*: c.7; speaks: c.12.

Molig, village N of Prada in the Castellana river valley renowned for its thermal waters; in *Rosselló,* c.6.

Moncayo, massif and mountain peak (2313 m / 7588 ft) W of Saragossa; in *La Maladeta,* c.4.

Monegals, valley in Ripollès county; according to legend, site of an ancient Benedictine monastery whose monks founded Santa Maria de Ripoll; invoked by Oliba: c.12.

Mont, pre-Pyrenean mountain range in W Alt Empordà, whose sanctuary of *La Mare de Déu del Mont* atop its highest peak (1115 m / 3658 ft) dates from the early fourteenth century, built on the site of a former castle; Verdaguer spent the summers of 1884-85 at the sanctuary composing part of *Canigó*; and the faerie of Banyoles: c.6.

Mont Blanc, western Europe's highest mountain, compared with La Maladeta in *La Maladeta*, c.4.

Montbram, mountain valley on the north side of the Alberes, sloping from the tower of Maçana to the west and presided to the east by a pinnacle atop which lie the ruins of the castle of Montbram (cited thirteenth century); in the *Passage of Hannibal*, c.7.

Montferrer, village in Vallespir above the Tec river valley at the SE base of the Canigó massif whose Romanesque church of Santa Maria dates from the tenth century; bellsmiths of: c.5; c.8.

Montgrony, or Mogrony, mountain range in W Ripollès noted for its sanctuary of *Santa Maria de Montgrony* erected below a cliff and, on the plateau above, the church devoted to Saint Peter, *Sant Pere de Montgrony*; and the faerie of Ribes: c.6.

Montner, village in NW Rosselló (built on the site of a former medieval castle); the watchtower, reconstructed, was first cited in 1275: c.2.

Montoliu, mountain peak (2660 m / 8727 ft) in NE La Vall d'Aran: c.4.

Montsent, mountain peak (2882 m / 9455 ft) in northern Pallars Jussà SSE of Els Encantats: c.4.

Montserrat, massif of pipelike pinnacles rising 1224 m / 4015 ft NW of Barcelona and site of the sanctuary *La Mare de Déu de Montserrat* and the Benedictine monastery *Santa Maria de Montserrat* founded in 1023 by Bishop Oliba, Catalonia's foremost devotional shrine; the patroness of Catalonia is represented by a Romanesque likeness carved in wood dating from the late twelfth or early thirteenth century: c.4.

Moor(s), c.5; in *Lampegia*, c.7; c.8, 10.

Moor's Grotto, the, (Cat. *La Balma del Moro*, Fr. *La Cabane del Moro*), dolmen situated NE of the village of Llauró (Fr. *Llauro*) on the N slopes of the Tec river valley: c.8.

Mount Vallier, (Fr. *Mont Valièr*), peak (2838 m / 9311 ft) in SW Ariège (France) named after Saint Vallier who, Verdaguer notes, was bishop of Couserans until 1505, and according to tradition planted a marble cross on the summit: c.4; in *Noguera and Garona*, c.7.

Moses, depicted on the portal of Santa Maria de Ripoll: c.11; invoked by chorus of monks: c.12.

Naiads, fresh-water nymphs of rivers, lakes, springs and fountains: c.3; in *Rosselló*, c.6.

Nature, personified: c.3, 9.

Nereids, sea nymphs, daughers of Nereus and Doris; in *Rosselló*, c.6.

Neto, (today, Aneto), highest peak of all Catalan-speaking territories rising 3404 m / 11,168 ft in La Maladeta massif in Osca (Sp. *Huesca*): c.4; Celtiberian god: in *La Maladeta*, c.4.

Noedes, (Fr. *Nohèdes*), village in Conflent, evoked by the faerie of Galamús: c.12.

Noguera, name of four rivers in Pallars Sobirà: La Noguera Pallaresa, La Noguera de Cardós and La Noguera de Vallferrera, which joins La Noguera de Tor (Pallars Sobirà); the Noguera river valleys of Pallars: c.4; La Noguera Pallaresa ('restless Noguera'): c.4; in *Noguera and Garona*, c.7 (see *Noguera Pallaresa*).

Noguera and Garona, tale of two rivers told by the faerie of Fontargent: c.7.

Noguera Pallaresa, river emerging in the Beret massif (E La Vall d'Aran), running southward through Pallars Sobirà, Pallars Jussà and Noguera counties, and flowing into the Segre; in *Noguera and Garona*, c.7 (see *Noguera and Garona*).

Noufonts, mountain peak (2864 m / 9396 ft) NE of Núria separating Ripollès from Conflent (France): c.4.

November, invoked by departing faeries: c.12.

Núria, mountain valley (1960 m / 6430 ft) nestled against the Pyrenees at the northern end of Ripollès County where Puigmal, Noufonts, Finestrelles and other peaks partially encircling the valley separate it from Northern Catalonia (France), site of Catalonia's most popular devotional shrine after Montserrat; according to tradition, a pilgrim from Dalmatia, Amadeus – who searched in vain for the likeness of the Virgin and Child left by St. Giles of Athens who had formerly preached the Gospel to shepherds in the valley – erected the chapel devoted to the Blessed Mother of Núria, the likeness to be discovered shortly after Amadeus's departure: c.4; invoked by the faerie of Ribes, by the provosts of Núria and Font-romeu: c.12.

Ogier, (Cat. *Otger Català*), legendary governor of Aquitaine at the sound of whose horn there came nine horsemen from nine lands to the cave at Montgrony (see *Montgrony*) where he was recovering from battle wounds and together they vowed to drive back the Saracens, conquering Pallars, La Vall d'Aran, Capcir and Cerdanya; according to tradition, his origins can be traced to *castrum Catalaunicum* at Châlons-sur-Marne, giving rise to the popular etymology of 'Catalonia'; cited in *Gesta Karoli Magni ad Carcassonam et Narbonam* (1418); died fighting against the Saracens at Castelló d'Empúries; his sword given to Tallaferro by St. William: c.5; his shade appears to the monks in *Eixalada*, c.9.

Oliba, (bishop of Elna and Vic, abbot of Ripoll and Montserrat; c.971-1046), brother of Tallaferro and Guifre II: c.2; presides Gentil's burial: c.9; undertakes the reconstruction of Santa Maria de Ripoll and founds Sant Martí del Canigó: c.11; drives the faeries from the mountain, plants the Cross of Canigó at the summit: c.12.

Olot, capital of the modern county of La Garrotxa, E of Ripollès, bound by early feudal ties to the monasteries of Camprodon and Besalú: c.4.

Òpol, castle now in ruins on the hill behind the village of Òpol (Fr. *Opoul-Perillós*), in the northern tip of Rosselló, reconstructed in the thirteenth century by the Crown of Aragon: c.2.

Ordino, river valley in W Andorra: c.4; c.12.

Orieja, (Fr. *Ariège*), river valley NE of Andorra; and the faerie of Fontargent: c.6.

Orla, mountain peak (2617 m / 8586 ft) in La Vall d'Aran along the NE border with Ariège (France): c.4.

Orseolo, Peter, doge of Venice (976-978) who ended his days as a monk at Cuixà, canonized by Oliba; in *Eixalada*, c.9; speaks: c.12; epilogue.

Ossau, (or Aussau), mountain peak (2884 m / 9462 ft) in the Pyrenées-Atlantiques (France) W of Vignemale; compared with La Maladeta in *La Maladeta*, c.4.

Osseja, village in SE Cerdanya (cited 947); in the *Passage of Hannibal*, c.7.

pabordes, traditional dance in honor of the Virgin Mary in which a decorative glass or earthen jug with several spouts (Cat. *almorratxa*) is used to shower the square with fragrant water: c.6.

Pailer Rock, (Cat. *Roc Pailer*), one of two high rocks in the upper Llitera valley N of Canigó; meeting place of witches: c.2.

Pallars, historic county in NW Catalonia dating from the early tenth century, modern counties of Pallars Sobirà and Pallars Jussà: c.4.

Panissars, mountain pass between La Jonquera and El Portús (Vallespir): c.5; the ruins of the tenth-century monastery Santa Maria de Panissars straddle the French border W of the fortress of Bellaguarda.

Passage of Hannibal, tale told by the faerie of Mirmanda, who saw Hannibal crossing the Pyrenees with his army en route to Italy during the Second Punic War: c.7.

Patroness, the Blessed Mother, patroness of Santa Maria del Camp, invoked by monks of the monastery: c.12 (see *Camp*).

Pebbles, the, (Cat. *el Palet or Palets*), or Roland's Pebbles, two oblong monolithic tables that stood side by side SE of Batera: c.8; Verdaguer notes: '*I went to see them three years ago, searching the steep scrubland as for a needle in a haystack, only to find them in pieces, having been hammered to bits by road gangs "having a little fun."'*

Pedraforca, mountain branching SE from the central Cadí range in Berguedà County, named 'forked rock' after its jutting peaks separated by erosion: c.4.

Pelayo, (?-737), Visigothic lord and first king of Asturias, whose victory over the Saracens at Covadonga ushered in the Christian conquest of Muslim Spain: in *La Maladeta*, c.4.

Pelós, c.2 (see *Guifré el Pelós*).

Pena, sanctuary of *Nostra Senyora de Pena*, overlooking the Aglí; in *Rosselló*, c.6; Verdaguer notes: '*a young woman fleeing the Saracens leapt from a cliff, unharmed, thanks to the intercession of the Virgin Mary, which is why the cliff is called the Damsel's Leap.*'

Pentina, mountainous woodlands (1913 m / 6276 ft) SW of Rubió: c.4.

Pere Pinya, legendary founder of Perpinyà: in *Rosselló*, c.6.

Perpinyà, (Fr. *Perpignan*), present-day capital of Rosselló and bishopric (see *Elna*) since the nineteenth century; legendary founding by Pere Pinya: in *Rosselló*, c.6.

Pessons, twelve lakes in SE Andorra; invoked by the hermit of Meritxell: c.12.

Pharaoh, invoked by chorus of monks: c.12.

Philistines, in *La Maladeta*, c.4.

Phoenicians, founded settlements in Rosselló: in *Rosselló*, c.6.

Picos de Europa, massif (2642 m / 8667 ft) along the Asturias-Cantabria border in the Cantabrian range: in *La Maladeta*, c.4.

Pla d'Anyella, sloping plateau (1840 m / 6036 ft) in Ripollès W of Toses: c.4.

Pla de Beret, plateau (1860 m / 6100 ft) in E La Vall d'Aran sloping eastward up to the Beret massif and draining, northward, into the Noguera Pallaresa, southward into the Garona: c.4 (see *Beret*).

Pla Guillem, broad plateau (2300 m / 7545 ft) SW of the Canigó massif named after St. William of Combret; c.4.

Planès, village in the upper Tet river valley, Alta Cerdanya (France) NE of Llívia; in *Lampegia*, c.7; in *Eixalada*, c.9.

Pomero, or Pomèro, mountain peak (2489 m / 8166 ft) separating Benasc from La Vall d'Aran: c.4.

Portvendres, (Fr. *Port-Vendres*), seabord town in SE Rosselló: c.1; Tallaferro attacks Saracens holding the town: c.5.

Potosí, city and region of Bolivia renowned for its precious metal mines: c.3.

Prada, (Fr. *Prades*), city in Conflent on the Tet, given to Count Sunifred of Urgell and Cerdanya by Charles the Bald in 843; in *Rosselló*, c.6; sacked by Saracens: c.7; in *Eixalada*, c.9; epilogue.

Proficiscere, anima christiana, (Onward, Christian soul), prayer for a departing soul; spoken by chorus of monks: c.12.

Provence, c.11; invoked by monks from the monastery of Camp: c.12.

Puig d'Alba,[1] (today, Pic d'Alba), mountain peak (3107 m / 10,193 ft) at the northern end of La Maladeta massif: in *La Maladeta*, c.4.

Puig d'Alba,[2] mountain peak (2764 m / 9068 ft) in SE Ariège (France): c.4.

Puig Neulós, highest peak (1263 m / 4143 ft) in the Alberes range, separating Alt Empordà and Rosselló: c.5; and the faerie of Banyoles: 6.

Puigmal, mountain peak (2910 m / 9547 ft) W of Núria and highest in the eastern Pyrenees after Carlit: c.4.

Puigpedrós, mountain peak (2911 m / 9550 ft) NNW of Meranges separating Baixa Cerdanya and Alta Cerdanya (France); in *Eixalada*, c.9.

Pyrenees, at sunset, in *A Saint John's Bouquet*: c.1; compared to a magnolia, as throne for Canigó: c.2; c.3; seen from Flordeneu's flying chariot, compared to a cedar in *La Maladeta*, compared to a 'malformed serpent': c.4; c.5; various descriptions in *Rosselló*, throne to Flordeneu: c.6; in the *Passage of Hannibal*, c.7; in *Eixalada*, c.9; various descriptions, Núria and Font-romeu as Regina of, invoked by Oliba, by final chorus: c.12; in poem's final line: epilogue.

Queralbs, town in Ripollès County on the Freser S of Núria; and the faerie of Ribes: c.6.

Queribús, or Querbús, castle (*castell de Busensi*, 1017) belonging to the historic county of Besalú from the eleventh to thirteenth centuries situated ENE of Sant Pau de Fenollet (France): c.8.

Ramon I of Cerdanya, (also Ramon Guifré, ?-1068), son of Guifre and Guisla; c.9.

Red Sea, depicted on the portal of Santa Maria de Ripoll: c.11.

Reiners, former castle (*castrum de Rayners*, 1307) on the hilltop N of the modern village of Reiners (Fr. *Reynès*): c.8.

Requesens, early medieval sanctuary, and later, site of the Castle of Requesens, situated on a hilltop (511 m / 1676 ft) on the southern slopes of Puig Neulós; c.5.

Rhone, river, in the *Passage of Hannibal*, c.7; Tallaferro drowns: c.11.

Rià, c.2 (see *Arrià*); Count of Rià, aka Guifre II of Cerdanya, whose castle was in nearby Rià, founder of Sant Martí del Canigó; alternatively, Sunifred II of Cerdanya, founder of Sant Miquel de Cuixà, in which case the tower of Sant Martí speaks erroneously in lines 61-70 of the epilogue (on this question see Pinyol 2002, 183n, and Torrents 1995, 220).

Ribes, or Ribes de Freser, town in central Ripollès where the Rigard flows into the Freser: c.4; and the faerie of Ribes: c.6, 12.

Ribes, caves of, situated in the village of Campelles SW of Ribes de Freser; the caves in the cliff-face, rich in legend, are renowned as a hideout for fleeing Christians: c.6; invoked by the faerie of Ribes: c.12.

Ribes, faerie of, tells of the caves of Ribes and presents Gentil with a golden crown: c.6; speaks: c.12.

Ripoll, site of Benedictine monastery, Santa Maria de Ripoll, refounded by Oliba in the early eleventh century and capital city of the modern county of Ripollès on the Freser; compared with Mirmanda: c.6; and the faerie of Ribes: c.6; c.9; reconstruction of monastery: c.11; invoked by Oliba: c.12.

Roca Colom, mountain peak (2507 m / 8225 ft) along the Northern Catalonian border at the SW end of the range connecting the Canigó massif to the main Pyrenean trunk: c.8.

Rocabertí, castle of, today a few walls, entry gate, tower and chapel remain of the castle atop a cliff NNE of La Jonquera, rebuilt in the twelfth century: c.5.

Rocacorba, mountain range (994 m / 3261 ft) in NW Gironès County SW of Lake Banyoles; and the faerie of Banyoles: c.6.

Rock of the Two Spell-Struck Hunters, c.4 (see *Els Encantats*).

Rojà, mountain ridge extending SW from Verdes Pass: c.4.

Roland, (?-778), (Cat. *Rotllà*, from the Germanic *hrod*, 'glory,' and *land*), hero of Charlemagne's court whose death in battle at Roncevaux is related in the Old French epic *La chanson de Roland* and whose legendary exploits are further related by Ariosto in *Orlando Furioso*; appears frequently in Pyrenean legend: Roland's grave in *La Maladeta*, c.4; Roland's mace: c.5, and in *Noguera and Garona*, c.7; Roland and megalithic dolmens: c.8 (see *Roland's mace*).

Roland's mace, name given to the iron shaft five meters high (16 ft) standing in the main square of Maçanet de Cabrenys: c.5; according to legend, Roland hurled the shaft from the Castle of Cabrera, or from Ceret, saying: *'Allà on la meva maça caurà, Maçanet de Cabrenys serà'* ('The spot where my mace alights, will be called Maçanet de Cabrenys'), giving rise to the popular etymology of 'Maçanet' (*small mace*); separately, on the plain of Esterri (near the River Escrita, affluent of the Noguera Pallaresa), a piece of iron jutting up 70 cm (2 ft) from the ground – another of the legendary maces wielded by Roland; in c.5, and in *Noguera and Garona*, c.7.

Romans, 'lay aside their gladii': in the *Passage of Hannibal*, c.7 (see *Spaniards*).

Rome, in the *Passage of Hannibal*, c.7; c.11; invoked by chorus of monks: c.12.

Romuald, also Romualdo, accompanied Orseolo to Cuixà, later returning to Italy to found the Camaldolese Benedictine monastery (1012) near Arezzo; in *Eixalada*, c.9; speaks: c.12; epilogue.

Romulus, Pere Pinya compared to: in *Rosselló*, c.6.

Roses, (from the Greek *Rhodes*) seabord city in the modern county of Alt Empordà where the Alberes and Balmeta ranges branch off from the Pyrenees and descend to the Mediterranean; its Benedictine monastery, now in ruins, dates from the sixth century; in *A Saint John's Bouquet*, c.1; c.4.

Roses, faerie of, tells of the sea and presents Gentil with a bouquet of pearls: c.6; speaks: c.12.

Rosselló, (Fr. *Roussillon*), derived from 'Ruscino' (see below), present-day county of Northern Catalonia between Conflent and the Mediterranean; in a broader sense, all of Northern Catalonia (counties annexed by France in 1659); historic county of Northern (French) Catalonia established in the ninth century: c.2, 5; in *Rosselló*, c.6; in the *Passage of Hannibal*, viewed by Guifre atop Canigó: c.7; Guifre surveys the Saracen advance: c.8; in *Eixalada*, c.9; c.11; invoked by St. Damasus: c.12.

Rosselló, tale of Rosselló told by Flordeneu: c.6.

Rubió, mountain hamlet in Pallars Sobirà SW of Sant Joan de l'Erm: c.4.

Ruscino, Iberian settlement in Perpinyà dating from at least the sixth century BC: c.2; in *Rosselló*, c.6; in the *Passage of Hannibal*, c.7.

Sahara, c.2; in the *passage of Hannibal*, c.7.

Saint Anthony, invoked by the hermit of Galamús: c.12.

Saint Benedict, appears to Guifre: c.11.

Saint Damasus, (Cat. *Damàs*), celebrated pope (366-384) who according to a medieval tradition hailed from the village of Argelaguer, near Besalú; speaks: c.12.

Saint Emery, early ninth-century Benedictine monk who according to legend tamed the dragon terrorizing Banyoles; invoked by the monks of Banyoles: c.12.

Saint Eulària, or Eulàlia, fourth-century martyr and patroness of Barcelona; speaks: c.12.

Saint Galdric, or Saint Galderic, born near Toulouse c.830, patron saint of farmers in Rosselló (and formerly throughout Catalonia) part of whose relics are preserved at Sant Martí del Canigó: c.9.

Saint George, (Cat. *Sant Jordi*), fourth-century martyr from Cappadocia and patron saint of knights whose popularity in Catalonia dates from the eighth century: c.5; Oliba consecrated an altar to Saint George in Santa Maria de Ripoll in 1022.

Saint John's Bouquet, A, (Cat. '*Lo ram santjoanenc*'), poem in c.1; Verdaguer notes the Vallespir custom of placing a small bouquet above the entrance to homes for the feast of St. John on June 24: '*In one of the farmhouses of Vallespir…lived a maiden as beautiful as a bouquet. A young suitor recently hired in the local iron mills took a liking to her, and she encouraged him though she didn't know where he came from…on the feast of St. John, as was the custom, she set out early before Holy Mass to gather some good fortune [in finding a husband], and trusting in the saint, she picked some herbs of his namesake and displayed them in the form of a cross above her door. Returning from Mass, she met her young man along the road and…he accompanied her home. She went inside and seeing he didn't follow she invited him to sit on the stool just inside the door…and as he refused she asked him why. He replied that he didn't care for the herbs he saw at the door. Curious about her suitor, she offered to remove the intimidating herbs if he told her his name. He replied that he was the Devil (God keep us safe!), who cannot withhold his name when asked. Not only did the maiden leave the bouquet intact, she related the encounter to all the neighboring maidens and the following year the Saint John's bouquet was seen on all the doors in Vallespir.*'

Saint Lucian and Saint Marcian, (Cat. *Sant Llucià, Sant Marcià*), wayward youths converted to Christianity who suffered martyrs' deaths in Vic under the persecution of Decius (r.249-251); speak: c.12.

Saint Marcian, (see *Saint Lucian and Saint Marcian*).

Saint Martin, (Cat. *Sant Martí*), Saint Martin of Tours (c.316-397), Roman soldier, missionary and founder of first monasteries in Gaul, Bishop of Tours (371), and patron saint of knights; according to legend, as a young soldier he once shared his cape with a pauper: c.1; invoked by Talleferro while held prisoner off Cotlliure: c.5.

Saint Michael, (Cat. *Sant Miquel*), likeness recovered by Eixalada monks at the site where Sant Miquel de Cuixà was to be founded: in *Eixalada*, c.9.

Saint Narcissus, (Cat. *Sant Narcís*), patron of Girona; according to legend, bishop of Augsburg who suffered a martyr's death in Girona in 307; speaks: c.12.

Saint Paul, depicted on the portal of Santa Maria de Ripoll: c.11; invoked by chorus of monks: c.12.

Saint Peter, depicted on the portal of Santa Maria de Ripoll: c.11; invoked by monks of Sant Pere de Roda, by chorus of monks: c.12.

Saint Vincent, speaks: c.12; Verdaguer notes: '*Saint Vincent of Cotlliure, who upon entering Catalonia suffered a martyr's death under Datian on 19 April 303.*'

Saint William, (Cat. *Sant Guillem de Combret*), ninth- or tenth-century ascetic of the hermitage Sant Guillem de Combret high in the Comalada valley on the southern slopes of the Canigó massif; and the iron bell: c.5; and the cursed stone: c.11; speaks: c.12; Verdaguer heard the legends of the iron bell and the cursed stone while sojourning in La Presta during the summers of 1879-80.

Salfort, or Sallafort, peak E of Puig Neulós separating Alt Empordà and Rosselló: c.5.

Salòria, mountain peak (2789 m / 9150 ft) in Pallars Sobirà County W of Andorra: c.4.

Salses, (Fr. *Salses de Château*), the modern village in WNW Rosselló was built on the site of the medieval castle (first cited 1275); the reconstructed tower stands today: c.2; in the *Passage of Hannibal*, c.7.

Samson, compared with Gentil: c.7.

Sant Joan de l'Erm, medieval sanctuary (now in ruins) S of the Santa Magdalena: c.4; according to legend, Arnau of Castellbò brought the Holy Grail there from Béziers in 1208.

Sant Llorenç, or Sant Llorenç de Cerdans, (Fr. *Saint-Laurent-de-Cerdans*), town in S Vallespir NE of the Castle of Cabrenç: c.5.

Sant Martí, hermitage on the NW base of the Canigó massif; c.1, 9.

Sant Martí del Canigó, Benedictine monastery founded in 1007 by Guifre and Oliba; in Guifre's farewell to Guisla: c.10; construction: c.11; personified: epilogue.

Sant Miquel de Cuixà, (Fr. *Saint Michel de Cuxa*), Benedictine monastery near Codalet, founded in 879, administered today by Montserrat Abbey; legendary origins: c.9; invoked by St. Romuald and St. Marinus, by St. Orseolo: c.12; one of its two bell towers fallen, personified: epilogue.

Sant Ou, or Saint Eudald, popular fifth-century convert and martyr, perhaps originally from Toulouse, whose relics were brought from Portvendres to Ripoll in 978; (see *Hole of Sant Ou*): c.6.

Sant Pau de Fenolleda, today Sant Pau de Fenollet, (Fr. *Saint-Paul-de-Fenouillet*), town in the county of Fenolleda (WNW of Rosselló), whose older (tenth-century) Benedictine monastery was given by Bernat I 'Tallaferro' to Sant Miquel de Cuixà in the year 1000: c.6.

Sant Pere de Roda, or Sant Pere de Rodes, Benedictine monastery devoted to St. Peter perched on the coastal mountains overlooking the Mediterranean at Cap de Creus; legend holds that Pope Boniface IV had St. Peter's relics sent from Rome (threatened by Chosroes II of Persia) to the Iberian coast for safekeeping, then ordered the construction of the abbey, invoked by the monks of Sant Pere de Roda: c.12.

Sant Vallier, c.4 (see *Mount Vallier*).

Santa Magdalena, or Romadiu, river flowing southwesterly in Alt Urgell and Pallars Sobirà N of Sant Joan de l'Erm then into the Noguera Pallaresa: c.4.

Saracen(s), c.1, 4, 5, 6; in *Lampegia*, c.7; c.12.

Segre, river emerging at 2000 m / 6560 ft near Puigmal and running northwesterly through Llívia then southwesterly through east-central Catalonia through the city of Lleida and flowing into the Ebre at Mequinensa: c.4; in *Noguera i Garona*, c.7; c.8.

Serrabona, eleventh-century priory near Bula d'Amunt (Fr. *Boule-d'Amont*), the early church was enlarged (1082) to accommodate an Augustinian priorate; reformed in the twelfth century, the preserved monastery stands today atop the ridge of the same name NE of the Canigó massif: c.8; in ruins: epilogue.

Setcases, mountain village on the River Ter in the upper Camprodon valley: c.8.

Setúria, high river valley in W Andorra: c.4.

Sícoris, Ibero-Latin name for the River Segre (see *Segre*): c.4; coins of gold from the Segre were minted in Lleida during Muslim rule.

Silva talem nulla profert / Fronde, flore, germine, (No forest has any [tree] with such foliage, blooms and buds), from the sixth-century hymn attributed to Venantius Fortunatus; spoken by chorus of saints among the clouds: c.12.

Sinai, in *La Maladeta*, c.4.

Sirac, or Cirac, village overlooking Rià where the castle of Sirac once stood: c.2; cave south of the village: c.6; Verdaguer notes: '*local lore has it that this cave once communicated with the cave of Bastera in Vilafranca*' (see *Bastera*).

Sodom, c.12 (see *Lot*).

Soldeu, village in Andorra at the southern end of the Incles river valley: c.12.

Solomon, depicted on the portal of Santa Maria de Ripoll: c.11.

Song of Gentil, Gentil's soliloquy: c.7.

Spain, in *La Maladeta*, c.4; the faerie of Mirmanda's mirror compared with 'the crown of Spain': c.6; in *Noguera and Garona*, c.7; invoked by chorus of monks, by St. Damasus: c.12.

Spaniard(s), 'Spaniards with long swords' in the *Passage of Hannibal*, c.7: according to Livy, the Romans thereafter adopted the *Iberian* sword, favored by Scipio; 'A Spaniard frenchified': the River Garona in *Noguera and Garona*, c.7.

Spanish March, generally accepted as the northern and eastern counties of Catalonia feudalized by Charlemagne as a Frankish defense zone under Catalan counts: c.4.

Syria, in *Lampegia*, c.7.

Tallaferro, (*tie-yuh-FAIR-oo*), Count Bernat I of Besalú, Vallespir, Fenollet, Ripoll and Urgell (c.970-1020), nickname from twelfth-century *Gesta comitum* chronicles of Ripoll, father of Gentil and brother of Guifre II and Oliba; forbids Gentil's love for Griselda: c.1; gathers militia to the defense of Elna, captured by Saracens, escapes from Cotlliure harbor: c.5; pursues Saracens: c.8; forgives Guifre: c.9; drowns in the Rhone: c.11; his spirit descends to meet Guifre's: c.12.

Tallaferro Hill, (Fr. *Taillefer*), above Portvendres (NE of Madaloc) from which Tallaferro launches his attack: c.5.

Talteüll, (Fr. *Tautavel*), watchtower standing SE of the village of Talteüll in NW Rosselló, cited in 1130 as *losa de Far*, reconstructed in the thirteenth century: c.2.

Tarascó, (Fr. *Tarascon*), town in Provence on the Rhone famed for its agricultural market: c.3.

Tarns, (Cat. *Els Estanyols*), small steep-banked pools at the source (2300 m / 7545 ft) of the River Cadí in the center of the Canigó massif: c.2; cloaked in fog by Flordeneu: c.8.

Taurinyà, or Torinyà, village in the valley of Balaig at the northern base of Canigó drained by the Llitera: c.2.

Tec, or El Tec (Fr. *Le Tech*), river emerging SW of the Canigó massif and flowing northeasterly through Vallespir and Rosselló into the Mediterranean S of Elna: c.1, 5; a string on the huge lyre formed by Rosselló: in *Rosselló*, c.6; Guifre pursues Gedhur up the river: c.8 (see *Ceret*).

Ter, river emerging in Ripollès county and running southeasterly into the Mediterranean E of Girona; the town of Ripoll lies where the Ter meets the Freser: c.12.

Tet, or La Tet (F. *La Têt*), river running NE through Conflent and Rosselló north of the Canigó massif and into the Mediterranean near Perpinyà: c.2, 3, 5; a string on the huge lyre formed by Rosselló, Pere Pinya follows the river: in *Rosselló*, c.6 (see *Pere Pinya*); the likeness of St. Michael is carried down the river: in *Eixalada*, c.9.

Thebaid, desert region of ancient Egypt known for its Christian hermits; invoked by the hermit of Galamús: c.12.

Tethys, a Titaness, daughter of Gaea by Uranus, wife (and sister) of Oceanus and mother of rivers; her ivory palace beneath Elna: in *Rosselló*, c.6.

Tiber, compared with the Tet in the legendary founding of Perpinyà: in *Rosselló*, c.6.

Titans, in *La Maladeta*, c.4.

Toses, mountain village in NW Ripollès: c.4.

Tortosa, city near the Ebre river delta; in *Noguera and Garona*, c.7.

Toulouse, in *Noguera and Garona*, c.7.

Tredòs, village in E La Vall d'Aran on the River Ruda, affluent of the Garona; in *Noguera and Garona*, c.7.

Tregurà, highest village (1425 m / 4675 ft) in the Camprodon valley, perched (325 m / 1066 ft) above the Ter: c.8.

Tretzevents, mountain peak (2731 m / 8959 ft) in the south-central Canigó massif N of the Comalada: c.2, 8, 9.

Tristany, or Tristaina, three mountain lakes (L. *tria stagna*) situated in NW

Andorra below Tristaina Peak (2876 m / 9435 ft) along the border with Ariège (France): c.4.

Trophies of Pompey, Roman monument commemorating Pompey's passage over the Pyrenees: c.5; Verdaguer notes that its remains may lie buried in the foundations of the seventeenth-century fortress of Bellaguarda SW of El Portús.

Tuïr, (Fr. *Thuir*), town in Rosselló whose twelfth-century church is devoted to Our Lady of Victory, in honor of Charlemagne's victory over the Saracens in Rosselló.

Ulldeter, spring (2390 m / 7841 ft) on the S side of the Pyrenean border separating Conflent and Ripollès: c.8.

Vale of Eina, (Cat. *Vall d'Eina*), river valley in Alta Cerdanya stretching NW of Eina Peak (2794 m / 9166 ft) which separates it from Núria to the south: c.4.

Valencia, capital of the Kingdom of Aragon, Catalonia and Valencia, which flourished under King James I (r.1213-1276), and modern capital of the Catalan-speaking Comunitat Autònoma de València: c.4.

Valira, main river of Andorra flowing southward into the Segre at La Seu d'Urgell: c.4; invoked by the hermit of Meritxell: c.12.

Vall d'Aran, La, modern county of Catalonia where Aranese (a variety of Occitan) is spoken (see *Viella*); Pyrenean valley E of La Maladeta: c.4; in *Noguera and Garona*, c.7.

Vallespir, county comprising the upper Tec river valley SW of Rosselló and SE of Conflent (see *Vallespir, faerie of*); and St. William's church: c.11; invoked by St. William: c.12.

Vallespir, faerie of, in the *Passage of Hannibal*, c.7.

Valmanya, or Vallmanya, village on the E side of the Canigó massif: c.8.

Venice, c.12 (see *Orseolo*).

Venus, invoked by monks of Sant Pere de Roda: c.12.

Verdes Pass, (Cat. *Collades Verdes*), mountain pass (2282 m / 7486 ft) beyond Pla Guillem SW of the Canigó massif: c.4.

Vesuvius, Mount, in *Eixalada*, c.9.

Vic, capital of the modern county of Osona, S of Ripollès: c. 4; bishopric since the sixth century, the diocese was restored following the Saracen offensive of the early eighth century; Oliba erected and consecrated in 1038 the Romanesque cathedral devoted to St. Peter.

Viella, (Aranese, *Vielha*), capital of La Vall d'Aran, situated on the Garona: c.4.

Vignemale, (or Vinhamala), massif (3303 m / 10,836 ft) in the west-central Pyrenees bordering France and Spain W of Catalonia; compared with La Maladeta in *La Maladeta*, c.4.

Vinçà, village on the River Tet below Prada, irrigated by streams running off the northern side of Canigó: c.8.

Virgin's Bridge, (Cat. *Pont de la Verge*), bridge across the Tec near Serrallonga (Fr. *Serralongue*): c.5.

Zeyan, Syrian chieftain who led the punitive expedition against Abu-Nezah; in *Lampegia*, c.7 (see *Abd ar-Rahman*).